Complete Taxation Guide to Canadian Real Estate Investing

Cherry Chan, CPA, CA

Cherry Chan, CPA, CA

Copyright © 2017 Cherry Chan

All .

ISBN:1545140022
ISBN-13: 9781545140024

Complete Taxation Guide to Canadian Real Estate Investing

◆ ◆ ◆

I have worked with Cherry for many years. She is incredibly bright, very personable and has a wide breath of knowledge resulting from her training as both a CPA and a Realtor. A unique combination of skill sets that is highly valuable.

Chris Dowding
Partner | Audit
Deloitte Private

◆ ◆ ◆

As an experienced real estate investor, I have to express my great appreciation for what Cherry does. She provides clear, sound and practical tax advice that allows me to focus on improving my portfolio's performance - and mine! She proactively advises me on structuring our various numbered companies and personal income (salary and dividend) to effectively plan our tax obligations ... Saving us tens of thousands of dollars. In addition to financial advice, she provided me with practical business and personal advice. Thanks, Cherry!

Monica Lee
Owner of commercial properties (plaza, mixed retail buildings, multi residential), student rentals, single family rentals, development land.

◆ ◆ ◆

Cherry excels at taking accounting questions and scenarios and breaking them down into plain English. It's a refreshing change to have someone so clearly outline different scenarios on matters that can often cause confusion for people.

Nick Karadza
Broker of Record
Rock Star Real Estate Inc., Brokerage

Cherry Chan, CPA, CA

♦ ♦ ♦

Cherry Chan's insights into accounting for real estate investors are must reads for me. Clear, direct and accurate, exactly what every investor needs.

Don R Campbell
Investor, Author and Philanthropist

♦ ♦ ♦

Why would you get advice that could be a lemon, when you could get advice from Cherry.

Quentin DSouza
Chief Education Officer
Durham Real Estate Investors Club

♦ ♦ ♦

Kutner Law LLP has worked with Cherry Chan and her clients for many years and have always found her to give clients excellent tax and business advice taking into account the client needs and assisting them to grow their portfolios in a tax efficient manner."

Howard Kutner, LLB, LLMA

Complete Taxation Guide to Canadian Real Estate Investing

❖❖❖

Cherry is the consummate professional and an expert in accounting for real estate professionals. She has a unique ability to distill accounting terms and strategies into the useful and relevant forms for us non-accountant types. Hands down, from page 1 on, the information in this book will allow you to make more strategic accounting decisions in your own life and business.

Ryan Hindmarsh
Leadership Development Coach
LMI Canada

❖❖❖

Cherry Chan's expertise has been invaluable in many ways, both for me personally, as well as for many of our clients. Her in depth knowledge of tax from a Real Estate perspective has been essential for enabling clients to grow their portfolio's much faster and more efficiently than if they were going at it alone. She is constantly up dating her knowledge of changes within the tax environment to ensure her clients are making the best decisions for their business. She is also a true expert on Real Estate corporate structures. She truly knows her stuff and I highly recommend her to anyone looking to purchase Real Estate or running a small business.

James Maggs
Real Estate Investor
Realtor

Cherry Chan, CPA, CA

Contents

Preface 9
   Who's this book for? 9
   Disclaimer 10
   Acknowledgement 11

Basic taxation 101 17
   Personal Tax 17
   Corporation tax 21
   Tax Integration 25
   Income versus Capital 27
   Ownership Structure 33
      Personal ownership/Sole proprietorship 33
      Partnership 34
      Corporation 35
      Joint venture 37

Real estate investment deductions 39
   Top ten deductions for real estate investors 39
   Membership 44
   Home office expense 48
   Meals & entertainment 54
   Automobile expense 58
      Keeping an autolog 58
      Deductible automobile expense 60

Complete Taxation Guide to Canadian Real Estate Investing

- Should I lease or buy? 60
  - What if I use my vehicle for both my self-employed business and my rental properties? 63
  - Purchasing a vehicle with your real estate corporation 63
- Startup costs 67
- Capital cost allowance 69
- Repairs & maintenance 72
- Gift cards 82

Principal residence 85
- Recent CRA Audit Initiatives on principal residence 88
- Renting out a basement or using a portion of home as business .. 92
- Cottage 95
- Little known 4 year extension on principal residence 98
- Preserving interest deductibility when converting Principal Residence to a rental property 100

Special cases 103
- Rent to own taxation 103
- Buying and selling new built 111
- HST on new builts 116
- Right or Wrong Things to Do Paying Your Contractors Cash 123
- Guide to AirBnB taxation 125
- Joint Venture Accounting 129

Corporations Talk 133

7 Questions to decide whether you should incorporate..............133

Examining the Pros & cons of 3 most common structures 140

    One corporation, multiple properties 140

    One corporation, one property 142

    Three tiered corporations 143

Commonly ask questions 145

    Where should I start?...145

    Will the tax savings be worthwhile for me to setup the 3 tiered corporation? When would it make sense?..............................146

    I have sufficient insurance coverage for the liability. I don't think corporations can help much to protect me..............................147

    Should you charge more than $30,000 of management fees in a 3 tiered corporation setting? 151

    Small business owners & real estate investors: 5 tips to structure your portfolio properly..152

    Transfer properties to corporation can be expensive 157

Would I setup a 3 tiered corporation myself?.............................161

Resources 165

Complete Taxation Guide to Canadian Real Estate Investing

Preface

Who's this book for?

Real estate is a powerful investment tool.

I started my investment journey before turning 30. I was a young Chartered Accountant, knew very little about investing.

I started by buying one student rental in my own name. In the same year, we bought two more student rentals with two different partners, also in our own names.

Even though I am a licensed accountant, I had little knowledge about real estate taxation on different strategies and structures.

I started researching, going back to textbooks, court cases and Canada Revenue Agency's website.

I work with hundreds of real estate investors, met with over a thousand of them.

This book, together with my weekly RealEstateTaxTips.ca newsletter, is written to provide you a starting guide about Canadian Real Estate Taxation.

Hopefully you will find the answer you need here.

Cherry Chan, CPA, CA

Disclaimer

I am not responsible for anything I say in this book.

That's always a fun comment to make at every presentation I started.

The truth is, tax planning is a personalized decision. It goes back to your own situation and what your priorities are. Sometimes it also goes back to your risk tolerance.

So, here we go – the proper disclaimer:

The information contained in this article is for general information purposes only. The information is provided by Cherry Chan and while we endeavour to keep the information up to date and correct, we make no representations or warranties of any kind, express or implied, about the completeness, accuracy, reliability, suitability or availability with respect to the article or the information, products, services, or related graphics contained on the presentation for any purpose. Any reliance you place on such information is therefore strictly at your own risk. In no event will we be liable for any loss or damage including without limitation, indirect or consequential loss or damage, or any loss or damage whatsoever arising from loss of data or profits arising out of, or in connection with, the use of this book.

Complete Taxation Guide to Canadian Real Estate Investing

Acknowledgement

For those of you who don't know, I was a young immigrant 15 years ago. We did study English in Hong Kong, but we never really conversed in English and used it outside of our exam paper.

I remembered being the only person that barely knew any English when we landed in Canada as a family. I communicated with the local custom when we first got out from the plane. I got the TTC bus map, took my family around the city to find a job in 2 weeks after we landed.

I also remembered that I couldn't understand a word when watching CP24. At the time Breakfast Television was on and I had no clue what they were saying at all on TV.

I knew some English, but I really had no idea.

Then I got into University of Waterloo. Living away from home opened my eyes up to a world of opportunity.

During frosh week, I was sitting right next to a Chinese looking girl and listening to her conversation with her friend. They were speaking so fast that I again didn't understand a word. Her name is Crystal.

I thought to myself – if only I can understand them one day.

Sure enough, we grew to become friends over the years and Crystal is one of my best Raptor buddies now. ☺

Cherry Chan, CPA, CA

For that, I dedicate this book to all the immigrants here. I came here when I was 17. If I could speak in front of over 660 people in my second language and wrote a book, you too can do that!

I was enrolled in the co-op program. This means that we didn't really get any summer holidays. We used up all of them for co-op work term, except first year.

During the first summer, we received an invitation to apply for a position at a Toronto based small accounting firm for the upcoming year.

I got hired immediately on the spot. The only catch was that it was a Chinese accounting firm and I had to waive my right to apply to any other accounting firms in second year.

But I got a job offer already. I signed it without putting much thought into it.

September came and it was the beginning of the second year. Big Five accounting firms all came in one night to do presentations to the entire year 2 class.

Everyone dressed up nicely and they all sounded very sophisticated. Almost everyone wanted to raise their hands to get into the Big Five.

I felt a bit bumped because I waived my right to apply. But well, I could always get into those Big Five firms later.

Turned out, these firms would interview many students for a coop job, as many as 50 students, not only limited to second year. But they would only hire 5 in total.

One female classmate also got an offer during this process from the same accounting firm as me. She was debating on whether she should accept the offer or go for the second round of coop matching process.

I liked her and strongly encouraged her to accept the offer.

Her boyfriend, also in the same program as us, said to her, "if you accept this offer, you will be perceived as a fob (short form for fresh off the boat) and you will never be employed by the big firms again."

His comment was not directed to me, but I was there listening to the whole conversation.

She and I ended up working together at the same accounting firm. We both moved onto different medium size firms after.

Mintz & Partners, the medium sized firm that I worked in, merged into Deloitte. I ended up working for Deloitte for a couple of years in their Private Company Services Group.

As with this boyfriend, he got the first interview by the Big Four but never got accepted. He ended up working for a smaller Chinese accounting firm in a different city.

Truth to be told, I've only come across a couple of incidents that I was looked down on because I wasn't born and raised in Canada. I was only called a FOB by my people, never once a different skin colour.

For that, I dedicate this book to everyone who had people looking down on you and considered you as a FOB. If I can write a book and

educate people in a second language and be truly proud to be a Canadian, these name callings mean very little.

I finished Master of Accounting at Waterloo and went on to write my Chartered Accountancy final exam. Thanks to my study partners, Irene & Jason, who kept me extremely focus, I got onto the Honour Roll. Top 50 in Canada, and top 10 in Ontario.

For that, I dedicate this book to my parents and my two study partners. Without them, I would not achieve this type of academic success in my life.

That was one of the biggest achievement in my life. I was in a relationship with someone who was so much more successful and accomplished in his life than a new grad like me.

I totally lost myself in this relationship.

We had some happy time together. We travelled often and I was living a comfortable life.

I could choose not to work and still lived comfortably. But there was this emptiness in me.

I was told that wearing heels would make me more feminine and putting on make up would be make me prettier. I was happy to oblige.

I was smart, regarded highly at work. But whatever I did in my career, it was never good and never good enough. It was never my success but his success.

Complete Taxation Guide to Canadian Real Estate Investing

For that, I dedicate this book to the women out there who think that they need another person to validate themselves and gives them the confidence they need, I was one of you. All you need is yourself. We are all worth it.

Getting out from a comfortable relationship was not easy. I did it.

I worked for a company that was owned by a guy who constantly abused his employees and sexually harassed most female staff.

I worked there for a year and realized that I was worth way more than putting up with that type of abuse.

For that, I dedicate this book to everyone who are abused and harassed in different forms or shapes, stand up for yourself. If I can make it work, so can you!

Finally, I met Erwin Szeto, who introduced me to the world of real estate investing and the freedom I got owning my own business.

He always kicked my ass every time I had any self doubts. He refused to listen to me. (He could some times be an ass, believe it or not!)

Of course, he also gave me two beautiful babies. And I was once led to believe that I couldn't get pregnant!

I now own my accounting practice and a couple of real estate investments, things that I've never thought it would be possible.

I could even teach people a thing or two about real estate investing these days!

Cherry Chan, CPA, CA

For that, I dedicate this book to my wonderful husband and my two beautiful babies, Robin & Bruce. I am trying very hard to be an excellent wife, a great mom and a role model for my children. Sure enough, I struggle at times and there're many mistakes made and to be made but I will never be able to do this, and the rest of my life, without all of you.

Thank you!

Cherry

Complete Taxation Guide to Canadian Real Estate Investing

Basic taxation 101

Before we talk about any real estate tax tips, it is worthwhile to start with some tax fundamentals. Let's examine the basic principles to our Canadian tax system.

Personal Tax

The Canadian personal tax system is a progressive tax system. This means that the more you make, the more you get taxed on.

The chart below shows you marginal tax rates for Canadians residing in Ontario in 2016:

Income range	Marginal tax rate
$45,000 - $73,000	30%
$73,000 - $91,000	34%
$91,000 - $140,000	43%
$140,000 - $150,000	46%
$150,000 - $200,000	48%
$200,000 - $220,000	52%
$220,000 and above	54%

Source: http://www.taxtips.ca/taxrates/on.htm

I have simplified the above chart to summarize all major marginal tax rates for you. There are additional income range and marginal tax rates below $45,000. There are also basic personal tax credits that each of you are entitled.

The best way to explain this system is to use an example. Let's say a person earns an income of $80,000.

For someone who has only a basic income tax credit, the person is responsible to pay $6,632 tax on his first $45,000.

Income range	Marginal tax rate	Tax liability
Below $45,000		6,632
$45,000 - $73,000	30%	8,400 (($73,000 - $45,000) x 30%)
$73,000 - $91,000	34%	$2,380 (($80,000 - $73,000) X 34%)
Total tax liability		$17,412
Average tax rate		22%

Depending on how much you make, different part of your income is being taxed at different marginal tax rate.

For someone who earns $80,000 job income, the first $45,000 of his income is roughly taxed at 15%. The next $28,000 is taxed at 30%. The last $7,000 of his pay check is taxed at 34%.

But his overall tax rate is different.

There're two main concepts here: *average tax rate* and *marginal tax rates*.

Average tax rate is calculated by dividing your total tax liability over your taxable income.

As an example, for a single person who makes a taxable income of $100,000, he pays $24,979 in 2016 in Ontario.

His average tax rate is therefore 25% (24,979/100,000).

Marginal tax rate is the tax rate being applied to your highest chunk of taxable income.

For someone who makes $100,000 income, his boss decides to give him a raise of $10,000. This $10,000 is taxed at his marginal tax rate, 43%. So he gets taxed of 43% of this additional $10,000 that he makes.

His total overall tax liability = $24,978.74 + $4,300 = $29,278.74.

His new average tax rate is $29,278.74/$110,000 = 26.62%.

Yes, a 10% raise on your gross income will only give you an after tax increase of 57%. Boo! ☹

Similarly, when you contribute to your Registered Retirement Saving Plans (RRSPs), all contribution is considered a tax deduction. Tax deduction gets taken off from your top marginal tax rate.

Say with this new raise, you earn $110,000 job income. You want to save some tax by contributing to your RRSP for $10,000.

This $10,000 is coming off from the top marginal tax rate. You can get a refund of $4,300 back if your employer deducts the personal income tax appropriately.

Why are these two definitions important?

As a real estate investor, your rental income is subject to tax. If you purchase one property which earns you a net rental income of $10,000 for the year, depending on what your marginal tax rate is, your rental income is added to your regular income including your job income and get taxed at the corresponding marginal tax rate.

Using the example earlier, for someone who already earns $110,000 job income, the additional rental income of $10,000 is taxed at 43%, an additional $4,300 of tax liability.

Adding to his tax from his job income, his tax liability is now $33,579 ($29,279 + $4,300).

His average tax liability is 28%.

You just cannot simply take what your income tax withheld on your paycheck and divide it by how much you get taxed to come up with your tax rate. You get taxed more than your average tax rate!

Recognizing what the marginal tax rate on the additional rental income also allows you to make an informed decision to choose over the ownership structure.

Complete Taxation Guide to Canadian Real Estate Investing

Corporation tax

There are many type of corporation tax, public corporations, private corporations, Canadian Controlled Private Corporation (CCPC), foreign corporations.

For the scope of our audience, we focus our energy describing the taxation on CCPC.

From the real estate investment context, let's discuss two important concepts – Active Business Income and Passive income (Specified Investment Business (SIB)).

Active income is income earned from a business source, including any income incidental to the business.[1]

Specified Investment Business is a business with the principal purpose of deriving income from property, including interest, dividends, rents, or royalties.[1]

Active business income concept is important because the active business income entitles the business owner for the Small Business Deduction (SBD) for the first $500,000 net income.

This essentially means that the business tax you pay inside a corporation is only 15% in Ontario (10.5% Federal and 4.5% Ontario).

WHAT?!

Yep! It is 15%. Not 30%, not 34% or 54%. It is 15%.

---

[1] http://www.cra-arc.gc.ca/E/pub/tg/t4012/t4012-06-e.html#P2883_209821

Instead of having a job working for someone else earning $100,000 income, you can open up a store and start selling widgets. Say you earn $100,000 in your business inside a corporation; you are only responsible to pay 15% tax on this $100,000.

Instead of paying $24,979 personal tax, you now pay $15,000 inside a corporation.

Who wouldn't do this all day long?

But Active Business Income does not include SIB income. Specified Investment Business is a business with the principal purpose of deriving income from property, including interest, dividends, rents, or royalties.[2]

Specified Investment Business is often referred to as passive income.

Rental income earned is not considered active business income. It is therefore subject to a different tax rate.

You can get out of this Specified Investment Business if your corporation hires more than 5 full time employees in the business throughout the year.

Passive income is subject to 50% tax rate. Approximately 30% goes into a notional account called Refundable Dividend Tax On Hand (RDTOH).

---

[2] http://www.cra-arc.gc.ca/E/pub/tg/t4012/t4012-06-e.html#P2883_209821

You can view this RDTOH account as a balance owed by CRA to you.

CRA gives a refund (calculated based on a formula) to the corporation when the corporation declares a taxable dividend to its shareholders.

Let's use an example to illustrate.

Say a corporation earns net rental income of $10,000 this year. The corporation has a tax payable of $5,400.

$3,400 of this tax payable goes to a notional account called RDTOH, meaning, CRA owes you up to $3,400 when the corporation declares the dividend to its shareholders.

The $3,400 balance can be carried forward indefinitely until a taxable dividend is declared.

The corporation can also trigger the refund in the same year by declaring a taxable dividend in the same year.

If the corporation chooses to declare a taxable dividend to the individual shareholders in the same year, triggering maximum refund of $3,400, the corporation's tax liability is only $2,000.

Over the long run, the corporation is taxed at 20% on its passive income earned.

Now, the catch is that the corporation has to declare a taxable dividend. A taxable dividend is then taxed in the hands of the individual shareholders.

Individual shareholders are responsible to pay personal tax on these dividends. Boo!

Depending on your personal income, you may or may not have another layer of tax payable.

For someone who has no other income in their personal tax, they can receive $35,000 dividend income by paying a small amount of Ontario Health Tax Premium. (Yep, they always catch you somewhere!)

Tax Integration

Canadian tax system is designed in a way that a taxpayer pays more or less the same amount of tax regardless how he decides to own his business, properties, or investments.

The concept behind that is that your tax payable is the same if you earn $100,000 in your own name versus earning $100,000 inside the corporation and retrieving all income via dividend immediately.

If you earn $100,000 personally, the tax payable is $24,979 (excluding any CPP implication).

If you earn $100,000 in the corporation (let's assume it is all active business income for now), you pay $15,000 corporation tax.

When you declare all remaining $85,000 as dividend to yourself, you have to pay personal tax on this income. The personal tax liability on $85,000, assuming that you don't have any other income, is $10,988.

Total tax liability = $15,000 + $10,988 = $25,988.

The idea is that this total tax liability $25,988 should be comparable to the tax liability you would otherwise owe personally ($24,979) if you were to own the business in your own name.

What this means is that there's absolutely no tax advantage owning your business/properties/investments through your corporation, *if you decide to take all the money out in the same year.*

What if you choose not to take the money out in the same year?

Say you only take only enough to cover your personal expense, $35,000 every year over the next few years.

You owe $563 each year for the next two years when you receive $35,000 per year and owe $nil the third year when you receive $15,000, with the assumption that you don't have any other income in your personal name.

Your personal tax liability for all 3 years is now dropped to $1,126.

Your overall tax liability is now $15,000 + $1,126 = $16,126.

If you earn the income personally in one year, it costs you $24,979.

A difference of $8,853. Who wouldn't take this all day long?

What if you also have some adult children who are in universities and colleges earning very little income? They can potentially receive the same $35K of dividend income from your corporation and pay very little tax.

There are different planning opportunities and flexibilities that are available via corporation. You need to consult a professional accountant to decide the planning strategies to lower your overall tax liability.

Income versus Capital

Another important concept that we have to learn is income versus capital.

If you earn $100,000 income personally, you are subject to $24,979 personal income tax.

If you earn $100,000 capital gain personally, only 50% is taxable. Therefore, $50,000 is taxable income and this results in roughly $9,000 tax liability (again, assuming that you don't have any other income).

That's a huge difference between the two.

Naturally, all taxpayers would like to argue that all income is capital and therefore paying less tax.

Now what determines whether the profit you make is considered income or capital? As cited in the court case *Ayala vs. the Queen [2008]*3,

"There is no criterion to determine with certainty whether a transaction leads to a capital gain or business income. Each situation is a specific case to be analyzed in light of the facts.

[10] Among the criteria developed by the case law, the following are of note:

i. *The nature of the property sold;*
ii. *The length of time the taxpayer was in possession as owner of the property;*
iii. *The frequency and number of operations carried out by the taxpayer;*

iv. *The improvements made by the taxpayer to the property;*

v. *The circumstances surrounding the sale of the property; and*

vi. *The taxpayer's intention at the time the property was acquired, as indicated by the taxpayer's actions.*

[11] In addition to these criteria, Canadian courts have developed the "secondary intention" criterion that may apply even when the taxpayer's main intention has been established as making a long-term investment. This criterion applies if, at the time the property was acquired, the taxpayer had considered the possibility of selling the property for a profit if the long-term investment project could not be achieved for whatever reason."[3]

Using this court case as an example, let's see how these criterions are applied:

- The taxpayer is a contractor that owns a renovating company
- The taxpayer acquired building 1 May 8, 2003 and sold it January 20, 2004. No rental income was reported during the period.
- He also acquired building 2 March 20, 2002 and sold it April 8, 2005. He incurred some amount of expenses for repairs.
- He acquired building 3 May 14, 2004 and sold it May 9, 2005, reported the transaction as capital gain on his personal tax return.

---

[3] http://decision.tcc-cci.gc.ca/tcc-cci/decisions/en/29747/1/document.do

Complete Taxation Guide to Canadian Real Estate Investing

Let's look at the criteria one by one.

i. *The nature of the property sold;*

   The property is a real estate property. You can hold a real estate property as a capital property to collect rent. You can also purchase this property and sell it quick for a profit.
   For building 1 & building 3, no rental income was generated. For building 2, the court case did not mention whether there was rental income reported.

ii. *The length of time the taxpayer was in possession as owner of the property;*

   The shorter the period the ownership, the more likely that these transactions are considered trading for a profit and hence should be reported as income.

   The taxpayer owned Building 1 for 8 months and 14 days.
   The taxpayer owned Building 2 for 3 years 19 days.
   The taxpayer owned Building 3 for 11 months and 25 days.

   For Building 1 and Building 3, the taxpayer owned both of them for less than a year. Arguably, for Building 2, the taxpayer could have kept the property for rental purpose given that the ownership period was much longer. The fact that the taxpayer only owns the properties for such a short period of time didn't help him to argue that the transaction is on the capital account.

Duration of ownership is only one factor that the court looks at. To achieve a comprehensive conclusion, the judge is required to look at all factors as a whole.

iii. *The frequency and number of operations carried out by the taxpayer;*

Obviously, the more transactions of a similar nature are completed by the taxpayers, the more likely the transactions are considered income.

Between 1996 to 2005 inclusively, the taxpayer transacted on 7 buildings for profit. He carried out the maintenance and repair work himself on the building sold.

In this particular case, the taxpayer's trading history also didn't help him to argue that he was selling the buildings for capital gain.

iv. *The improvements made by the taxpayer to the property;*

Generally speaking, when someone has the trading intention for a profit, he is more likely to renovate and repairs and "make it look nice" and sell it shortly after.

Therefore, the court looks at the amount of improvements being made by the taxpayer to the property.

In this case, the taxpayer spent $14K repairs on building 1 that's purchased at $142K. He spent $6K on building 2 that's purchased for $90K.

The extent of the renovation was not discussed in the court case. In my opinion, the amount of renovation

v. *The circumstances surrounding the sale of the property; and*

In this court case, during the initial interview, the taxpayer stated that his intention was to "sell it for profit". He later changed his story at the court level that he intended to purchase the property as a rental to supplement his income when he retired. Due to the fact that these houses were in bad location and could not be rented as expected, he decided to sell it.

The statement changed in this case and it didn't really help to prove that the taxpayer was trying to rent the property out but failed to do so.

vi. *The taxpayer's intention at the time the property was acquired, as indicated by the taxpayer's actions.*

Intention is always subjective. For a taxpayer to prove his intention, evidence must be provided that is consistent with the taxpayer's actions.

Sometimes this evidence includes their family party pictures and monthly utility bills. Documentation really matters when you are trying to prove your intention.

As mentioned above, taxpayer responded to CRA's auditor's enquiry by stating that his intention was to renovate it and sell it. This is the classic example of flipping a house for a quick profit.

The court analyzed all the case facts together with criteria and concluded that the taxpayers' actions demonstrated his intention was to purchase the property for a quick profit. Hence, the court dismissed the appeal.

As a quick recap, flipping for a profit should always be considered as income. Flipping, if done inside the corporation, is active business income. Flipping is not Specified Investment Business and hence is considered active business income.

100% of the income is taxable, but only subject to 15%.

Complete Taxation Guide to Canadian Real Estate Investing

Ownership Structure

Personal ownership/Sole proprietorship

Sole proprietorship is the simplest form of ownership. You can simply start up a business or own a property without any registrations (you may still need to register your business depending on what you are doing).

Income from your business or property are then recorded in your personal tax returns. You are eligible to deduct reasonable expenses that you incur for earning the income.

If you earn business income, you're then required to contribute to both employer and employee's portion of Canada Pension Plan. This is often computed as part of your personal tax return.

Your tax return for being self-employed is due June 15, but the tax payable is due April 30.

Pros

- Cheapest form of ownership to setup and its simple to setup
- Any losses generated from either your business or properties can be used to offset against other income
- It's also easier to keep track of all your income and expenses. You are not required to have a business bank accounts and can simply take money out from the business any time you want.

Cons

- Much higher tax rate if you are making big money. Highest tax rates in Ontario is 54%. But the first $500K for Canadian Controlled Private Corporation (CCPC) is only subject to 15% tax rate.
- Limited ability to split income with your spouse.
- Unlimited liability. If the business get sued, the sole proprietor is personally liable for all the liabilities. Creditors can even jeopardize your own principal residence.
- No continuity of business. If sole proprietor passes away,

Partnership

When more than one person operate and own a business together, you form a partnership.

Like sole proprietorship, each partner is required to report his share of business or property income individually in his personal tax return.

It's often simple to operate.

Like sole proprietorship, each partner's tax return is due June 15 but the tax liability is due April 30 of the subsequent year.

Pros

- Similar to Sole Proprietorship, it's the simplest and cheapest form to setup.
- It's also relatively simple to keep track of cash flow, income and expenses. You can take out the cash from the business without much tax concerns.

- If you own the business with your spouse, you can split income with him/her.
- Any losses generated from the partnership can also be offset against other sources of income to lower your personal tax liability.

Cons

- Once ownership percentage is established, there's no flexibility in terms of how to change it subsequently.
- No continuity. Partnership doesn't exist anymore if one partner passes away.
- Unlimited liability - All partners are jointly liable for the action of any partner in the business. If one partner makes a bad business decision, every partner's personal assets can be at risk.
- Like sole proprietorship, if you earn significant income in the partnership, you can be subject to a much higher rate than earning income in a corporation.

Corporation

Corporation is considered a separate legal entity in the eyes of law. This means that you need to maintain proper record of the corporation whenever you put money in and take money out of it. You will also need to register your corporation

Pros

- Limited liability protection: Corporation is considered a separate legal entity. It can be sued on its own.
- With proper setup, you can split income with your lower income spouse and adult family members.

- You can also split income by paying your family based on the services they provide to the corporation. The compensation must be reasonable for the services they provide.
- Enjoy lower tax rate if you are earning active business income lower than $500,000 inside a CCPC. Tax rate is only 15% and you are able to use higher after tax dollars for investment.
- If you do decide to sell the business in the future, you can potentially sell the shares and enjoy a capital gain exemption for around $800,000, provided that the business qualifies as small business corporation.

Cons

- Cost to setup the corporation is relatively high. Legal fees to set it up can range from $1,500 to $2,500.
- Higher maintenance cost: Generally speaking, the cost of filing a corporation tax return and preparing the financial statements are more expensive than that of personal tax return. Business bank account charges are often higher than personal account bank fees.
- Separate banks and records must be established. Money withdrawn by the owners from the business must be properly accounted for. More often than not, there's tax implication every time money is being withdrawn.
- If you generate a loss inside the corporation, you can carry the losses forward for 20 years but you cannot use it to offset other income earned in the shareholders' personal tax return.

When should you incorporate to own your business?

Complete Taxation Guide to Canadian Real Estate Investing

This is often the million dollar question in all real estate investors, business owners and realtors mind.

For real estate investors, although you cannot enjoy the 15% active business rate (please refer to this blog post regarding how rental income is taxed inside a corporation http://realestatetaxtips.ca/use-corporation-lower-tax-liability/), you can still use the corporation to split income with your lower family members and liability protection.

For small business owners, incorporation provide the liability protection that you would not otherwise get and significant tax advantage. If you don't need all your cash flow from your business, it is often a great way to save and invest within the corporate structure.

For realtors, you may think that incorporation isn't even an option for you. But the reality is that you can bypass the system and setup a corporation by operating a mini brokerage. You too can also enjoy the significant tax advantage within a CCPC.

Truth is, incorporation is a personal choice and it should be determined based on your personal situation. Consult a professional to make an informed decision.

Joint venture

Joint venture is very similar to partnership. The biggest difference is that when you own your business or rental portfolio in a partnership, the capital cost allowance is claimed at the partnership level.

This means that the partnership determines the amount of capital cost allowance the partnership would claim.

If the partnership has only rental properties, and the partnership is incurring a rental loss in current year, no capital cost allowance can be claimed.

The individual partner may still have net rental income in his overall portfolio, but he cannot claim any more capital cost allowance on the properties owned inside the partnership to reduce his other net rental income to zero.

On the other hand, if the joint venture is formed instead, the same individual partner can choose to claim capital cost allowance on his portion of the asset against to reduce the rental income.

Thus, joint venture provides more flexibility.

Both joint venture and partnership can be formed by a combination of corporations or individuals. Depending on the participants, the filing requirements can be quite different.

Make sure you speak to a professional before making the decision between joint venture and partnership.

Real estate investment deductions

Top ten deductions for real estate investors

When you are a real estate investor, you are operating a business. Operating a business means that you are allowed to deduct all reasonable expenses incurred for the purpose of earning the income, subject to a bunch of exceptions.

Many of the expenses you can deduct are self-explanatory. Below are the top ten one that you should not miss.

1. Mortgage interest, not the mortgage principal

Many real estate investors think cash flow as their net income and they think that they get taxed on their net cash flow.

Monthly mortgage payment consists of mortgage interest and principal pay down. Mortgage interest is a deductible expense but principal pay down is not.

The breakdown between the two can usually be found on your annual mortgage statement you receive at the beginning of next year.

When you estimate the tax liability owing, you need to add your net cash flow to the mortgage paydown to compute your taxable income.

2. Insurance

Insurance coverage for rental properties is different than the home that you live in. Make sure you notify the insurance company about the change of use and that appropriate coverage is taken.

Generally speaking, insurance premiums on rental properties are more expensive than your personal home.

3. Advertising

Any advertising cost incurred for the purpose of renting out the property is deductible. This includes all the Kijiji ad costs, 'for rent' signs that you purchase from Home Depot or specifically made for your property, etc.

4. Property management fees / commission you paid to fill the property

If you hire a property manager or use a realtor to fill the property for you, these are all deductible expenses. Make sure you get the invoice from them to support your expense.

5. Repairs & maintenance

Repairs & maintenance are generally deductible expenses. The tricky part is to determine whether an expense incurred should be capitalized or should be expensed. If you paint the house, generally speaking it is a deductible current year expense. If you pay for the stamp concrete for your driveway which did not exist before, this will be capitalized and appropriate capital cost allowance can be taken on it.

Repairs & maintenance is one of the grey area that few people can understand. See subsequent section for detail discussion about this deduction.

6. Property taxes and utilities

Municipal property taxes and utilities are generally deductible against the rental income. One of the most missed property tax and utilities deduction is at the year of purchase or the year of sale. Some of the adjustments are handled by the lawyers and many investors would miss these deductions.

Specifically for investors who converted their primary residence to a rental property, only the expenses related to the rental period would be deductible.

7. Financing charge

Financing charge is usually one of the most missed deductions for real estate investors. Some real estate investors incur mortgage insurance expense or finder fees for their mortgages. These expenses can be deductible over a period of time but a lot of real estate investors miss it.

8. Auto mileage

This one is tricky. Different criteria apply if you own one property versus when you own more than one property.

For investors who only own one property, you are only allowed to deduct motor vehicle expenses if

- The rental property is in the same general area that you live in
- You do repairs & maintenance for your property
- You have vehicle expenses to transfer tools & materials to the property

But you cannot deduct the expenses you incur for the purpose of collect rent if you have only one property.

Now for investors who own more than one rental properties, on top of the expenses incurred for repairs & maintenance and transferring tools & materials as mentioned above, you can also deduct the following expenses:

- Collect rents
- Supervise repairs
- Generally manage the properties

To qualify for the multiple properties criteria, they must have at least two different locations than your principal residence. This means that if you rent out your basement apartment and have one single family detached home as rental property, you still cannot deduction any expenses incurred for collection of rent, supervision of repairs and general management of the properties.

See subsequent discussion on how to document and deduct automobile expense.

9. Capital cost allowance

Capital cost allowance is the tax term Canada Revenue Agency uses to represent the wear and tear on the building. It is a deferral mechanism allowed by CRA to defer the income on your properties until the year you sell it.

When you sell it, all the deductions taken throughout the year have to be reported as income.

See subsequent discussion on how to document and deduct automobile expense.

10. Line of credit interest

Many real estate investors start out by refinancing their own home to obtain the downpayment of their real estate investment.

Interest incurred on loans used for investment purpose is deductible.

Complete Taxation Guide to Canadian Real Estate Investing

Interest incurred on loans used for personal purpose is not deductible.

If you only have one line of credit and you use this line of credit to buy a new rental property and fund your family trip to Disney, only the interest incurred on the portion related to the rental property is deductible.

When you subsequently pay down this line of credit, you are paying down both personal and investment portion together. You cannot simply claim that the repayment is used to paydown your Disney trip.

Repayment is proportional to both investment use and personal use.

So as interest incurred.

The best practice is to setup two separate line of credits.

One for personal use and the other one for investment/business use.

When you have extra cash to repay your line of credit, repay the personal use line of credit first, as interest incurred on this line of credit is not deductible.

You can continue to deduct interest incurred on the investment line of credit.

As a general rule of thumb, expenses incurred for the purpose of earning income are deductible subject to a list of exceptions in the Income Tax Act.

There are some expenses specific to real estate investors. Some are deductible. Some, I would say, are less likely to be allowed.

Membership

I am a regular attendee to various real estate education seminars. My favourite one is Rock Star Member Event hosted by the Karadza brothers and Real Estate Investment Network's Authentic Real Estate Course.

I remember how I was fully blown away by the science and research done behind the presentations and the strategies that they teach.

There are so many tips and tricks you can learn.

Even with 6 years of investing experience, I still learn new things every time I attend these real estate meetings.

It was almost 10 years ago that my mom decided that it was time to move back to Hong Kong.

She has a detached house in Toronto rented out to tenants. I have been the designated property manager that takes care of the property since then.

Before I met Erwin a few years ago, I didn't know much about how to manage a property.

Complete Taxation Guide to Canadian Real Estate Investing

I advertised strictly on one mainstream Chinese newspaper in their classified ad section with the logic that a few Chinese families would be suitable tenants.

It was vacant for a few months before a middle aged Chinese guy finally committed to rent it.

We were all relieved.

He refused to put his name on the lease. He gave me his wife's driver license from Montreal.

He also didn't provide post dated cheques. He liked to pay everything with cash.

He claimed that he had sold his Chinese fast food restaurant in Montreal and moved to Toronto to have a new life.

We were desperate and I didn't know any better. I didn't do any background checks, didn't ask for T4 or employment letter, and of course I also didn't do any reference check.

When he paid rent on a monthly basis, he insisted in coming out to pay me by cash. We would meet in this parking lot of a brewery factory right by my townhouse complex in Etobicoke at midnight so he could give me a stack of cash. The exchange in the middle of the night just made me feel like we were trading something illegal!

I was always worried about my personal safety as well.

Other than the midnight rent collection in the dimmed parking lot, he wasn't too bad of a tenant.

One time his girlfriend's ex-boyfriend came out to break his windshield glass and the police were called.

He missed a couple of months rent at the end before he decided to leave the place without covering any of the water charge. (City of Toronto would not allow tenants to be on the water bill unfortunately.)

Even after he moved out, this ex-boyfriend still came to the house harassing my new tenants thinking he could get a hold of her.

That's before I met Erwin and got exposed to a wealth of real estate education.

This house is going to be available in the market again in May.

This time I know better. I know how to advertise and market it a lot better. I also learned to screen tenants and how to be a lot more selective. Hopefully we can get my mom a better tenant.

These education courses are the reasons why we buy houses. They gave us the road map to succeed in real estate investing.

The Income Tax Act allows all expenses that are incurred for the purpose of earning income to be deductible, subject to a list of exceptions.

Based on this criteria, all these education courses and membership fees we incurred would definitely qualify as a deduction against the rental income we receive.

We attend these seminars, we learn and we apply what they teach to buy houses and build a larger portfolio. We earn the rent because of what we learn there.

BUT some CRA auditors do not necessarily agree with this.

They don't see how these educational expenses would be an expense incurred for the purpose of earning rental income and hence disallow the claim.

Of course, we can always take it to the court when this happens. But for the time and headache involved, it's just not worth it.

Bottom line – I would still deduct the membership given that it is incurred for the purpose of investing, but always keep in mind there is a risk involved in deducting it.

What if you incurred these courses a while before you purchase any rental property? This just makes it a lot harder to claim the cause-and-effect relationship between your investment and the education you get.

Home office expense

The criteria to deduct home office expense can be quite confusing.

Let's look at the criteria for deductions.

Criteria for deductions

You are eligible to deduct home office expense as long as you meet one of the criteria below:

- Your home office is the *principal place of business*; or
- You use the space *only to earn business income* and you use it on *a regular and ongoing basis* to meet your clients, customers, or patients

Principal place of business

If you have more than one place to operate your business, your home office must be the main location.

This means that as a realtor, you may have a room in your home where you make all your sales calls, prepare all your paperwork and perform bookkeeping functions, but you are indeed conducting the deals at different houses.

This means that if you are a real estate investor, you may have a room in your home where you do all the bookkeeping, scout investment properties, prepare N4 notice to evict your tenants and advertise your properties for rent.

You are allowed to use this same room for personal use, like playing online video games, but this room is the principal place of business.

Or: Only to earn business income on a regular and ongoing basis

If you qualify under the second criteria, the home office space must be used exclusively to earn business income. This means that personal use is not allowed in this place.

On top of the exclusive use of the home office space, you also need to use it to meet clients on a regular and continuous basis.

If you are a realtor that only meets your clients in your home office once or twice a month, unfortunately it does not count as "regular and ongoing basis".

If you are a real estate investor that does not meet your tenants/clients in your home office at all (most landlords I know do not like their tenants to know where they live), chances are you probably cannot qualify to claim home office expense under this criteria.

What can you deduct?

Now, let's assume that you qualify with one of the criteria above, what can you deduct?

You can deduct the following expenses:

- Maintenance costs such as heat, home insurance, electricity, and cleaning materials.
- Property taxes
- Mortgage Interest
- Home internet
- Repairs
- Capital cost allowance

If you rent, you can deduct rent.

You can deduct part of the expenses that are related to running your business. This can be calculated based on the size of your home office in relation to the size of your home.

More often than not, a taxpayer would come to me and say that I would like to deduct 20% of my home office expense. He may have a number in mind that he would like to reduce his taxes by and hence come up with the 20%. But the reality is, you need to prove that the 20% you claim is reasonable.

If you have a house that 2,000 square feet, 20% is 400 sf. Ask yourself if your home office size is 20% of your home.

Deductions must be based on a reasonable basis. If your office size is not 400 sf, you can't simply claim 20% because you like the number 20%.

Deducting capital cost allowance against your principal residence also may not be a good idea if you are planning to claim principal residence exemption. Consult a professional accountant before claiming CCA.

What do you have to keep?

Similar to all the deductions, documentation matters.

You will need to keep all the invoices for all your utilities cost, property taxes, insurance, mortgage statement, internet expense and repairs.

If you rent, you will need to keep a copy of your lease agreement and proof of rent payment/receipts from landlord.

You will also need to keep the floor plan for your residence so you can provide proof that the 20% of home office expense you deduct is reasonable.

Limitation on deductions

Few people actually know that there's a limitation on home office expense deduction.

You can only claim home office expense to the extent of the business income you earn.

Say you earn $100,000 gross revenue and incur $20,000 expense, your net income is $80K. You can claim up to $80K of home office expense.

Say you only earn $10,000 gross revenue and incur $11,000 of expense, you have a net loss of $1,000. You cannot claim any home office expense you've incurred during the year.

However, you are allowed to carry forward any undeducted home office expense to future years for deductions.

Deducting home office expense against rental income

Canada Revenue Agency released a new income tax folio (a new tax interpretation) on Business Use of Home expense February 1, 2017.

It provided detail explanations and examples on the criteria to qualify to claim home office expense as detailed in my previous blog post.

It also specifically called out the expenses incurred in earning income from property.

GREAT NEWS!

If you earn non-business rental income, you **are eligible to claim home office expense.**

I have detailed the criteria that a taxpayer must meet to be eligible to claim home office expense above.

Specifically, a taxpayer can only deduct the home office expense if

- The work space is the principal place of business or
- The work space is used exclusively to earn business income and used on a regular and continuous basis for meeting clients of the business

This Income Tax Folio specifically says that when taxpayers are earning non-business rental income, they **do not need to meet these criteria**.

That's great news for real estate investors!

Furthermore, I mentioned previously that a taxpayer cannot use the home office expense to create a loss against his business income.

This **will NOT apply** to real estate investors earning non-business rental income.

Meaning – you can deduct home office expense even if you have a rental loss.

You can also deduct home office expense even if it means you have net rental loss afterwards.

Of course, similar to all other deductions, the expense must be reasonable. You are still required to keep a floor plan of your house, keep all your receipts for insurance, maintenance, mortgage interest, utilities, etc. to calculate the home office expense.

Now we have a CRA document calling out how to deduct home office expense against property income!

And now when we are questioned by CRA auditors why we are deducting home office expense against property income, we have this document to point to!

Meals & entertainment

To qualify as a deduction (even 50% deduction), you are required to incur the expense for the purpose of earning the business/property income.

So if you take your clients out for lunch, that can be a deductible meal.

If you take your parents out for lunch and they are not your clients, that lunch is not a deductible expense.

Deductible amount can be lower than what you spent!

Most savvy business people are aware that meals & entertainment expenses are only 50% deductible.

Few people know that only 50% of the reasonable amount is deductible.

An example is that you take your top client out and he loves wine. You ended up spending $10,000 on a dinner with a few bottles of expense vintage opened. A typical dinner would cost, say $1,000.

CRA can technically limit your deduction to 50% of the reasonable amount at $1,000 and disallow the claim of the $10,000.

Solo meals are generally not deductible

Many investors ask me this question before. Can I deduct my meals when I am on the road to see properties or visit my clients?

General rule of thumb is that, if you are eating all by yourself, chances are, the meals are not deductible.

As an employee, you may qualify to deduct 100% of it if your employer reimburses your meals and include it as part of your salary.

If your employer doesn't reimburse your meal and you are under an employment contract and are required to work for more than 12 hours away from your regular work place.

But for most of entrepreneurs out there, solo meals are not deductible, unless you charge it back to your client specify that you are claiming the meals against them.

Otherwise, arrange to have lunch or dinner with a supplier or customer, this can improve your business relationship and you can deduct you meals too!

<u>Restaurant gift cards & grocery gift cards are only 50% deductible</u>

Christmas is getting close. Many of us use this opportunity to thank our clients/tenants by sending them gift cards.

Unfortunately restaurant gift cards and grocery store gift cards are only 50% deductible as the underlying products are food and meals.

<u>Meals included as part of the convention cost need to be taken out</u>

Recently, we signed up for a convention next year.

Included in the large convention fees that we pay, they include lunch and dinner.

Although the organizer never splits the price between attending the convention and providing the meals, we, as taxpayers, are supposed to estimate the cost of the lunch and dinner included.

Say convention fees = $2,000, inclusive of lunch & dinner for a two day event.

CRA deems $50 per day is paid and this amount is subject to the 50% limitation.

Deductible convention amount = $2,000 – $50 x 2 days = $1,900.

Deductible meals = $50 x 2 days x 50% = $50

Total deductible expense = $1,950

HST is also subject to the same 50% limitation

You can only claim the 50% of the HST you pay on meals against the HST you collect from your clients.

Say if you incur $100, 13% HST, total bill is $113.

Only $6.50 can be claim as a credit against your HST payable.

Whereas if you spend the same $100 plus HST on office expense, you are eligible to claim the full $13 HST you pay against the HST you collect from your sales.

Employees parties are 100% deductible up to 6 times a year

If you host a party and make it available to all your employees, you can deduct 100% of the expenses.

This includes company picnics and Christmas party up to a total of 6 times a year.

Documentation matters

Visa statements don't count.

Complete Taxation Guide to Canadian Real Estate Investing

Bank Statements don't count.

When you get audited, only the actual receipts count!

Keep the actual receipts.

Be diligent at the time when you incur the expense, write down on the receipts who you were with on the receipts. When you get audited 2 years down the road, chances are, you won't remember who you spent the time with!

Automobile expense

Deducting business use of automobile expense is allowed and often one of the most overlooked deductions.

To properly deduct automobile expense, the first thing you need to keep is an autolog.

Keeping an autolog

Whether you are a real estate investor, realtor, work in sales or own your own business, you want to make sure you keep a proper autolog to keep track of your mileage.

This helps you support the automobile expense claim against the income you are earning.

To keep a full logbook, this means that you are required to keep the following information in your logbook:

- Date
- Destination
- Reason for trip
- Distance travelled

I have taken the honour to create a sample for your reference.

Complete Taxation Guide to Canadian Real Estate Investing

Date	Destination	Reason for trip	KM driven
1/1/16	Beginning odometer reading		25,786km
1/6/16	Home Depot	Pick up supplies for rental property	39km
1/7/16	Unit A, 1st Student Rd., Hamilton	Drop off supplies	82km
1/8/16	Unit A, 1st Student Rd., Hamilton	Showings for potential tenants	82km
	...		
	...		
	...		
12/28/16	3rd Student Rd, Hamilton	Collect rent	78km
12/31/16	Ending odometer reading		38,172km

At the end of the year, you sum up the business use mileage, say 10,786km.

Business use % = 10,786km / (38,172km – 25,786km) = 87%

Therefore, 87% of your automobile expenses are deductible.

Yes, this is a big hassle to keep every single trip. The more you claim, the more documentation you are expected to keep.

And it doesn't end here with the log book.

Other evidence including the following information are expected to be kept substantiating the reasonability of your logbook:

- Maintenance record/invoice that shows the odometer reading on your vehicle
- Daily planner that shows addresses that you have visited
- Receipts that shows the date and purchase (such as Home Depot receipts, etc.)

And yes, your logbook would also need to be consistent with all other circumstantial evidence.

It's a lot of work to set it up right, but once you set it up right and there is no substantial change in your business usage, you may be able to keep a smaller logbook in the subsequent years.

Deductible automobile expense

Further to the autolog, you can deduct the following automobile expenses –

- Fuel and oil
- Interest
- Insurance
- License and registration
- Maintenance and repairs
- Any other expenses that are directly related to operating your vehicle (I usually include my 407ETR bill as other expenses)
- Lease payment or capital cost allowance

The total of these expenses are then prorated based on the business use mileage or rental use mileage for deduction purpose.

You can also deduct parking expense, but only business use and rental use parking expense are allowed to be deducted. No proration is necessary for parking expense.

Note that you are required to keep all the receipts and VISA statements do not count.

Should I lease or buy?

In addition to the expenses mentioned, you can also deduct the business portion of your auto lease payment or auto depreciation.

If you finance the purchase of your vehicle, the business portion of the interest expense can also be deductible.

Many investors and small business owners come to me and ask the question – should I lease a vehicle or should I buy?

Complete Taxation Guide to Canadian Real Estate Investing

There's really no magic answer. More often than not, you are offered a different deal when you lease and finance the purchase, as opposed to buying it out right.

You usually get a cash discount if you buy the car out right. It is more like a financial decision, rather than a tax question.

Nonetheless, let me explain to you how you deduct the purchase of vehicle below.

If you purchase the minivan that I proudly own –

Using the 8 passenger minivan as an example, assume the purchase price is $35,000 with HST 13% = $39,550. Lease rate is 2.99% and monthly lease payment is $559 including HST.

If you purchase a passenger vehicle, the maximum amount you can capitalize and depreciate is $30,000 + HST = $33,900. Similar to all capital assets, you are allowed to deduct the capital cost allowance (CCA) on the car. The rate of deduction allowed is 30% a year (1/2 year rule applied the year of acquisition and the year of sale).

Year 1 – maximum amount you can deduct $5,085 ($33,900 * 30% * ½)

Say in 2014 you drive a total of 10,000km using this car, of which, 3,000km is incurred for the purpose of earning rental income, you are allowed to deduct $5,085 * 3,000km / 10,000km = $1,525.50.

Year 2 – maximum CCA you can deduct is $8,645 (($33,900 – $5,085) * 30%)

Say in 2015 you drive a total of 20,000km using this van, out of which 7,500km is incurred for the purpose of earning rental income, you are allowed to deduct $8,645 * 7,500km / 20,000km = $3,421.88.

If you lease the minivan –

The maximum eligible leasing cost allowed to be deducted is $800 on a monthly basis.

A complicated formula is used to determine the maximum eligible leasing cost can be deducted on an annual basis. You can follow this example in Canada Revenue Agency's website (http://www.cra-arc.gc.ca/tx/bsnss/tpcs/slprtnr/bsnssxpnss/mtr/ddctbl/ls-eng.html).

In our example, the maximum we can deduct for the first year is $559 per month.

Year 1 – maximum eligible leasing cost that can be deducted is $559 * 6 = $3,354

Similarly, this needs to be adjusted for the usage specifically for the purpose of earning rental income. In 2014, you are allowed to deduct $3,354 * 3,000km / 10,000km = $1,006.20

Year 2 – maximum eligible leasing cost can be deducted is $559 * 12 = $6,708

Again, adjusting for the mileage used specifically for earning rental properties, maximum amount of eligible leasing cost you are allowed to deduct is $6,708 * 7,500km / 20,000km = $2,516.

What if I use my vehicle for both my self-employed business and my rental properties?

If you are also a small business owner, you drive the same car for your self-employed business and your rental properties, you are still eligible to deduct the business portion for your self-employed business and rental portion in your rental properties.

Say in year 1, you drive 5,000km for your self-employed business and 3,000km for your rental properties.

If you purchase the minivan, you can deduct CCA for $5,085 * 5,000km / 10,000km = $2,543 for your business. You can also deduct an additional CCA for $5,085 * 3,000km / 10,000km = $1,526 for your rental properties.

Administratively, you are required to record the mileage specifically used for your business and the mileage specifically used for your rental properties separately.

Purchasing a vehicle with your real estate corporation

When we found out we were expecting Bruce, the first thing we did to get prepared was trade in my small sedan for an 8-seat minivan.

It is a nice and highly rated van, big enough to accommodate our growing family but also affordable.

For business purposes, this van is excellent when my husband, Mr. Hamilton, takes clients out for tours to different cities.

At the time, we decided to purchase the car in our own name, as opposed to buying it in our corporations.

A few clients asked me if they should own their vehicles in their own names or their real estate corporations.

This really depends on how often you use your vehicles on your real estate portfolio.

Say you have a full time job and you don't have any other businesses besides your real estate portfolio, if you **purchase the car in your own name**, you have two ways to claim your expense through our real estate corporation.

You can claim it using the mileage method. All you would need to do is to keep a log book on the trips you made for your rental corporation. Based on the mileage you have driven, you are allowed to claim 55 cents on the first 5,000 km and 49 cents per km in 2015 on anything exceeding that from the corporation.

These allowance rates are posted on the CRA website and they are subject to change on an annual basis.

These rates are deemed reasonable and CRA would not question the reasonability of these rates. Meaning, that you don't need to keep track of the detail gas receipts, insurance expense and any other automobile expenses you have incurred. (Note, that a detailed log book is still required to prove that the mileage you are claiming is reasonable business use.)

For example, you incurred 6,000km to run your rental corporation. Based on the mileage allowance method, you can claim $3,240 ($0.55 x 5,000 + $0.49 x 1,000) from the corporation. The real estate corporation can deduct this $3,240 as an expense and yet you don't personally need to report it as income.

You can also choose to use the detailed method. This means that you will have to keep all the detailed receipts as noted in above, keep a log book, including the mileage you have driven your car for the full year. At the end of the year, prorate the expenses based on the mileage you have driven for business purpose in relation to the annual mileage you've driven.

We have another option – we **can own the vehicles in the corporation's name**, but this gets a whole lot more complicated!

From the corporation's point of view, the personal use portion of automobile expenses would not qualify for deduction. If you incur $10,000 of automobile expenses in total, and 70% of the time you use the vehicle for personal use, only $3,000 can be deducted as expense.

From your personal tax return point of view, because the car is available for you to use personally, you are receiving a benefit from the corporation. We call this a standby charge. You have to personally report it in your income and pay tax on this amount.

Depending on how often you drive the car for business purpose, the standby charge is calculated differently.

If you use the vehicle 70% of the time for personal purpose, the standby charge is calculated as 24% of the vehicle value (the purchase price of the vehicle). Say you purchase the vehicle for $40,000, the standby charge is $9,600 (24% x $40,000) annually.

If you used the vehicle 70% of the time for business purpose and the mileage you've driven for personal use is less than 1,667km per 30 day period or a total of 20,004km for the year, you may be able to reduce the standby charge.

The reduced standby charge is prorated by the percentage of your business use, the lesser the personal use, the lesser the standby charge.

Formula to calculate the reduced standby charge:

Personal use per kilometer × the number of months the car was available to you × standby charge calculated above

Oh yes! It can get pretty complicated!

We generally don't advise clients to own the car in the corporation unless the client used the car almost exclusively for business purpose.

Of course, the taxpayer will also have to keep proper record, especially a detailed mileage logbook, to ensure well supported deductions for your properties and standby charge.

Startup costs

Many investors had asked me when they would be able to start deducting expenses against their rental portfolio.

Many of them actually incurred a large amount of expenses upfront before they even own any properties.

Sometimes it can be as long as a year or two before they actually purchase their first property.

And they wonder if their expenses that they incurred on coaching and seminars from 2 years ago would be deductible.

Truth to be told, this is a grey area.

Whether a taxpayer is able to deduct expenses incurred prior to purchase of their property, it really comes back to when was the day the business started.

CRA considers that a business has begun whenever some significant activity is carried out.

Significant activity is either the regular activities that you would carry out to generate income OR an essential preliminary to normal operations.

To apply this criteria from a real estate investor perspective, significant activity can be the moment you sign a Buyer Agency Agreement with your Realtor to look for an investment property (this is an activity that you need to carry out to generate income).

Another example of significant activity can also be the moment that you submit your application for mortgage approval. You need to qualify for financing before you can purchase any properties. And mortgage pre-approval is the essential preliminary to normal operations.

If a taxpayer simply joins a real estate investment club to see if real estate investing is suitable for them, the costs of memberships to join the club would not be deductible.

On the flip side, if a taxpayer joins the real estate investment club and is actively looking for a property so that he can apply the knowledge that he learns, he's likely able to deduct the membership given that he's actively looking for a property.

When a taxpayer attends a $200 weekend workshop to "check it out", in which he also signs up for the $20,000 coach program that provides the step by step guide to invest, this can also be viewed as a significant activity to the start of your business. This can be viewed as the essential preliminary required to carry out the business.

Together with taking actions (actively looking for properties), this $20,000 coaching program can be a deductible expense. (But the $200 still isn't deductible since the taxpayer is just looking around).

The more evidence you can show that the significant activity related to the commencement of your business has happened, the earlier you can deduct the expenses.

And of course, it matters whether you actually purchase a property or not!

If you purchase the property, it's just so much easier to establish that your intention was always to have a business.

Capital cost allowance

Many investors ask me about whether they should deduct capital cost allowance against their rental income.

What exactly is capital cost allowance? Capital cost allowance represents the wear and tear of the building that the Income Tax Act allows you to deduct against your rental income.

Capital cost allowance can also be deducted against other capital assets (except land). The largest capital asset for a residential rental property is the building itself. You may also have some equipments, which have a different depreciation rate.

Capital cost allowance is a tax deferral mechanism, similar to RRSPs in a way. You deduct it against your rental income but you can only defer it till the year you sell your house.

When you sell your rental investment, you have to take the deductions you've made throughout the year into income and pay tax that year.

If you sell your rental property at a loss, depending on the magnitude of the loss, you may still need to report some deductions into your income the year you sell.

As a real estate investor, you may wonder if it is worthwhile to use this deferral mechanism.

If you own the properties in a corporation, it is _always_ worthwhile to deduct it against the rental income.

Reason behind it is simple. Passive income is taxed at 50% in the corporation initially. When you eventually sell the property and take all the years of capital cost allowance into income, it is still taxed at 50% then.

Cherry Chan, CPA, CA

A dollar in your pocket now is worth more than a dollar in your pocket 10 years from now when you sell your property. Why wouldn't you take the deferral opportunity now?

Note that you can only deduct capital cost allowance against the rental income. If you have a loss, you cannot use it to create a bigger loss.

Now if you own the properties in your personal names, the decision is not as clear.

This is simply because Canadians are taxed on a progressive tax rate system. The more you make personally, the more you get taxed.

Say if you make over $200,000 from your job income, your additional rental income of $10,000 is taxed at 52%.

In this case, similar to the corporation owned properties, I would definitely take the capital cost allowance to defer the income tax to the year you sell it.

Now say you are one of those accomplished investors who lives off their rental income and do not have any other job income, you have a few properties with total income before deducting CCA of $30,000. Would you take the capital cost allowance to defer the taxes?

With only $30,000 rental income, you are responsible for about $3,818 of taxes in 2015. This is equivalent to 12.73% tax rate.

If you take the CCA tax deferral every year for 10 years, you will be responsible for $300,000 income every year. The tax you have to pay for $300,000 is significantly higher than that of $30K every year.

Chances are, I would choose to pay the tax in current year and not take the deduction.

But again, it depends on the investor's personal situation and preference. Sometimes it makes more sense to defer the income and sometimes it does not.

Repairs & maintenance

As real estate investors, our real estate investment is our business. Our product is our houses. Our clients are our tenants. Our business partners include our lenders, local government officials, contractors and most understated – Canada Revenue Agency.

Like any other businesses, to increase marketability of our houses and attract the best tenants, we renovate and we upgrade our house.

Some of these repairs provide an immediate and short term value.

Some of these are considered improvements that provide long term value.

One of our biggest business partners, CRA, also looks at these repairs and improvements closely.

Specific rules are in place to assist us to determine whether an expense is considered repairs or improvements.

Before we get into the rules, let me just explain the tax impact between repairs and improvements.

Repair is a current expense, it generally reoccurs after a short period of time. It is deductible against your rental income the year it's occurred.

Therefore, it is considered 100% deductible.

Improvement is a capital expense. It provides long lasting benefits. It is capitalized as an asset. A taxpayer is allowed to claim the wear and tear on the asset against its rental income.

Complete Taxation Guide to Canadian Real Estate Investing

When the property is sold at a gain, these "wear and tear" you have taken over the year would have to be taken into income. This is called recapture. You can find my discussion about capital cost allowance in this previous blog post.

This improvement is also added to the adjusted cost base of the building for the purpose of calculating the capital gain.

Capital gain is currently half taxable. If you make $100,000 capital gain, only $50,000 is taxable.

In another word, if an expense is considered capital expense, this simply means only 50% is deductible.

Let's use an example to illustrate this concept.

	Current expense (repairs)	Capital expense (improvements)
Expense incurred	$10,000	$10,000
Tax treatment – year of incurring the expense	$10,000 deducted against rental income.	$10,000 is added to the cost of building. Taxpayer can deduct 4% (the depreciation rate allowed by CRA on building) capital cost allowance (CCA) on the undepreciated building cost. In this case, taxpayer can deduct $200 1st year ($10,000 x 4% x ½ year rule on year of acquisition).
	If owned personally with 40% marginal tax rate, deduction is equivalent to $4,000 tax savings.	Tax impact = $200 x 40% = $80.

Use the expenditure to create rental loss	A taxpayer can report this expense which can potentially create a rental loss. If properties owned personally, the rental loss can then be offset against your employment income and lower the overall taxes you pay.	A taxpayer cannot claim CCA to create a rental loss. These deductions are capped by the amount of rental income you report.
Tax deductions – years after	Nil	2nd year = ($10,000 – $200) x 4%= $392. 3rd year = ($10,000 – $200 – $392) x 4% = $376 4th year and onwards until the year of sale = follow the same calculation above.
Tax impact – year it is sold	Say you purchased the property for $300,000 including closing cost, and you sold the building for $400,000. You then report $400,000 – $300,000 = $100,000 capital gain. 50% of it is taxable, $50,000 is taxable at 40% marginal tax rate. Tax liability in year 4 = $20,000.	Taxpayer will have to include in his income the CCA deductions he's taken in 1st year to 3rd year. In this case, he will have to add $200 + $392 + $376 = $968 into income. In tax term, this $968 is called recapture. 40% taxable = $387.20. For the purpose of calculating the capital gain, the taxpayer will add the improvement cost to the purchase price of $300,000, to have a total of $310,000 as the capital cost. Capital gain is therefore $90,000 ($400,000 – $310,000), 50% taxable = $45,000. Tax payable = $18,000. Total tax payable in year 4 = $18,387.20.

Complete Taxation Guide to Canadian Real Estate Investing

Overall tax impact for 4 years	$4,000 tax savings in 1st year $20,000 tax liability in 4th year NET overall tax liability = $16,000	1st – 3rd year tax savings = $387.20 4th year tax liability = $18,387.20 Net overall tax liability = $18,000

Bottom line – because you get a bigger tax deduction against your income, taxpayers are motivated to claim an expense as repairs rather than improvements.

On the flip side, our business partner, CRA, has a different idea.

Although there are specific rules in the Income Tax Act laying out the criteria to determine one over another, many taxpayers still find themselves fighting with CRA at the court level to make a decision.

Of course, as real estate investors, we are motivated to claim everything as repairs. As our silent business partner, CRA is motivated to rule the expense as capital in nature.

The criteria to determine repairs versus capital are not always black and white. But let's go through them nonetheless so we have a basis for discussion.

Here are the four criteria to determine whether an expense is considered current or capital expenditure.

1. Does the expense provide a long-lasting benefit?

    Capital expense is considered to provide long lasting benefit while current expense is considered to reoccur after a short period of time.

    The example used on CRA's website is setting up vinyl siding on a wooden house – this is considered a capital expense. On the other hand, if you simply paint the wooden wall of the house, this is considered as a current expense.

In real life, almost all expenditures fall somewhere in between capital and current expense based on this definition.

2. Does the expense maintain or improve the property?

The example given on CRA's website is pretty clear cut. If you replace the wooden steps with concrete steps, it is considered capital expense.

If you simply repair the wooden steps, then it is considered current expense and therefore 100% deductible.

Now, as a savvy investor, you may wonder what if you simply replace the broken wooden steps with new wooden steps, should they be considered current expense or capital expense?

There is no improvement done to the property, you are simply replacing the current broken one with a new one so it is still safe. On the flip side, this can potentially be viewed as providing long lasting benefit and hence can be viewed as a capital expenditure instead.

And if this is viewed as providing long lasting benefit, then what else is excluded from providing long lasting benefit? Even a fresh coat of paint can be viewed as providing long lasting benefit.

So what can really be expensed?

3. Is the expense for a part of the property or for a separate asset?

CRA says that capital expenses are the ones incurred for new assets replacing existing assets that are within the property. In other words, if you are buying a new furnace to replace the old one, they are considered a separate class of asset and hence should be capitalized. For electrical rewiring, it is considered repairs of the building, as long as it does not improve the property beyond its original condition.

4. What is the value of expense?

This rule only applies if you cannot come to a conclusion based on the above three criteria.

Generally speaking, capital expenditure is much higher in relation to the value of the building whereas the current expense is not.

Having gone through all these criteria, you may still wonder whether the expenditures you have incurred is considered capital or repairs.

You may actually wonder if any of the expenditure to maintain the property can ever be considered as repairs, given the stringent rules CRA are applying.

It's not always black and white. It's almost always in the gray area.

These four little known exceptions help eliminate some of the confusion you may have.

1. Buying an older building

Many of us buy resale homes. Many of these houses need quite a bit of work before you can rent them out. Gutting the bathroom and kitchen, replacing the doors and hardwood flooring, scrapping off the old style wall paper and painting it with a new modern colour; anything you can imagine.

According to CRA, the work you have done to renovate to make it suitable for rent is considered capital in nature, even though some of them are usually treated as current expense.

If you are one of the investors who bought a 1950s bungalow and converted it into a legal duplex to rent them out, chances are majority of the expenses are considered capital in nature and hence not deductible against rental income.

2. Selling your property

As savvy real estate investors, to maximize the sale price of our rental property, sometimes we do a few things here and there to fix the house for better marketability.

If you are incurring the expenses solely for the purpose of selling your property, the expenses are considered capital expenditure.

However, to confuse us more, CRA specifically says that they will allow expenses to be deducted as current expense if they are necessary and you made them to the property before you decided to sell.
Whether an expense is considered necessary is up for interpretation. Whether you made the expense before you decide to sell again is subjective.

Make sure appropriate documentation is kept to support your position.

3. Soft costs relating to construction, renovation, or alteration

Soft costs include interest, legal fees, accounting fees and property taxes.

If you incur these soft costs related to the land, it can only be capitalized as cost to the building.

If you incur these soft costs related to the building, it can either be capitalized or expensed.

4. Modifications made to accommodate persons with disabilities

If you incur expenses to accommodate people with disabilities, even though the expenses can be considered capital outright, CRA specifically allows you to deduct these expenses immediately the year they are occurred.

Now that we've learned all the rules, let's answer the most common questions real estate investors have:

1. *"I am replacing my rental property's roof. Can I deduct it?"*

This depends. :)

If you are replacing shingles with shingles due to wear and tear, I would deduct the expense given that you are not improving shingles.

If you are replacing the shingles with metal roof, the expense would have to be capitalized.

One of my student rental properties used to have a flat roof on one side of the house, causing significant damage inside. We built a slanted roof on that side of the house. This is again a capitalized expense.

2. *"What about replacing hardwood floor?"*

Under normal circumstances, replacing hardwood flooring with hardwood flooring is considered a repair expense.

If you replace carpet with hardwood flooring, it is considered an improvement and hence should be capitalized.

If you replace the hardwood floor after buying the old building, based on exception 1 above, it is considered capital expense.

If you also replace the hardwood floor for the purpose of resale, based on exception 2 listed above, it is considered a capitalized expense.

3. *"How about building an in-law suite in the basement?"*

If the basement was empty before, the renovation costs should be capitalized.

If the basement was simply dated with bathroom and kitchen, no additional improvements were made. I would argue the expense is repairs, provided that it was not under the same situation mentioned in exception 1 above.

With that, I would also advise the investor to keep pictures of what was there in the basement prior to renovation. At the end of the day, you are the one that's responsible to provide the evidence to prove your case.

If you are converting a non-legalized basement suite to a legalized one, the costs incurred are considered an improvement to the property and hence should be a capitalized expense.

Hopefully these common examples help you to understand the rules a bit better.

Gift cards

We believe that if you treat people nice, most of the time, they will also treat you nice as well.

Whenever we visit our tenants, we always try to buy some treats or gift certificates for them to enjoy. Most of our tenants appreciate this gesture. And hopefully they will take good care of our houses.

As a landlord and taxpayer, you may wonder if these gift cards are tax deductible or not?

Generally speaking, any expenses you incur for the purpose of earning income are tax deductible subject to certain limitations.

Limitations, such as subsection 67.1(1), that reduces the meals and entertainment expenses to 50% deduction instead of 100% as a result of human consumptions of food or beverages or the enjoyment of entertainment.

This means that if you take your tenants out for dinner, only half of the meals are deductible. You can spend $50 for both of you, but only $25 is deductible. This is stated in the Income Tax Act to eliminate the personal enjoyment portion of your meals.

You may then wonder if you can deduct 100% of your meals expenses if you purchase restaurant gift cards entirely for the enjoyment of your tenants without any of your participation?

A taxpayer in 2006 had already brought this scenario to court (*The Queen v. Stapley*, 2006 DTC 6075). The taxpayer was a self employed real estate agent. The taxpayer often bought gift certificates for food and beverages and tickets of various sporting events to his clients. He did not attend the dinners and the sporting events and hence he deducted 100% of the costs.

Initially the Tax Court ruled in favour of the taxpayer, based on the fact that the purpose of subsection 67.1(1) was to eliminate the personal enjoyment component from the deductions and the taxpayer did not participate in any of these events.

Unfortunately, the Minister appealed the decision made by the Tax Court to the Federal Court of Appeal. Based on the literal translation of section 67.1(1), expenses for food, etc. are 50% deductible in respect of human consumption of food and beverages or the enjoyment of entertainment.

Just because the taxpayer did not get to enjoy the entertainment or the food and beverages, someone else did. And just because the objective of section 67.1(1) was meant to eliminate the personal enjoyment portion, the section was not written in such a way that it wouldn't be applied if there was no personal enjoyment.

The judge reluctantly ruled in favour of the Minister. This means that all the gift certificates issued from a restaurant would be 50% deductible, not 100%.

Furthermore, in 2014, Judicial and CRA Interpretations of Canada Tax Law and Transactional Implication stated that if the gift certificates are issued by the supermarket, a permanent establishment that is primarily engaged in selling food and beverages, section 67.1(1) applies and only 50% of the expenses incurred are deductible.

Say, you are buying a Home Depot gift card for the purpose of earning the property income, since Home Depot is not an establishment that is primarily engaged in selling food and beverages, you should be able to claim the expenses 100% deductions.

Make sure you purchase the proper giftcards so you are getting the best deduction for your money!

Principal residence

To qualify and claim the principal residence exemption, the following criteria must be met

- Property must be a housing unit that can include the following-
    - A house
    - An apartment building or unit in duplex (we will discuss this further in another blog post), apartment building or condo,
    - A cottage
    - Mobile home or houseboat
    - Leasehold interest or share of the capital stock of co-op housing corporation
- Ownership is required (you cannot claim principal residence exemption if you don't own the property)
- The unit must be acquired for the sole purpose of ordinarily inhabited in it
- Property must be a capital property
- Property must be designated as principal residence by the taxpayer

Simple rules, aren't they?

Say a taxpayer bought a lot with an old house in a nice neighborhood, his plan was to knock down the existing property and build a brand new house for him and his family to live in it. This process took 2 years to complete. He's able to finally move into the property in year three.

He decided to sell the property in year four to move back into his previous residence.

More often than not, this taxpayer would be under the impression that the full gain is sheltered because he lived in the property in year three and year four (partially) and hence nothing is being reported on his personal tax return.

Upon sale, this taxpayer or the taxpayer's accountant MUST undergo the "badge of trade" analysis to consider whether this property is a capital property.

"Badge of trade"

Meaning that if the taxpayer's intention is to sell the property for a quick profit, together with other corroborative evidence demonstrated by the taxpayer's behavior, the transaction can be considered as a business activity. The property is not a capital property as a result, the money earned from this property cannot be sheltered using principal residence exemption, despite the fact that he lived in the property before.

CRA and the tax court had requested analysis from the taxpayer or the taxpayer's accountant in recent court cases to support the conclusion of a transaction as capital property transaction. When the taxpayer was unable to provide the analysis, the tax court tended to side with CRA and concluded that this property wasn't a capital property. And hence principal residence exemption doesn't apply.

Say we concluded that the property is a capital property with the sole intent by the taxpayer to live there, he is still not qualified to shelter the entire gain.

During the construction period, in years one and two, the taxpayer did not live in the property, therefore the gain for those two years are not sheltered as part of the principal residence exemption.

If the taxpayer made $100,000 capital gain on this property, we first need to calculate the per year based on the number of years owning the property. In this case, it is $25K per year.

Since he only lived in the property in year three and year four, he is only allowed to designate years three and four as the principal residence.

The Income Tax Act formula allows you to shelter the two years that you designated, PLUS ONE more year worth of gain. A total of three years of gain.

Hence, $25,000 x 3 = $75,000 gain is sheltered.

The taxpayer is still liable for $25,000 of gain at the time of sale. 50% is taxable and he will have to be taxed for the $12,500 net capital gain.

Proper form must be filed together with your tax return to reflect the sheltered portion and the taxable portion.

Cherry Chan, CPA, CA

Recent CRA Audit Initiatives on principal residence

CRA has focused their energy on the residential real estate market for a while. (They should, given that many people made their wealth in the residential market.)

There are two parts of their initiatives. One is the claim of principal residence exemption. The second one is the HST rebate on new homes purchase.

I am going to talk about the audit initiative CRA has started on principal residence exemption for the last few years and what I've learned from attending various professional seminars.

A few investors asked me about the new requirement to report sale of principal residence.

Few taxpayers actually understand that you can only qualify to claim principal residence exemption on a particular property if that property is a "capital property", even if you truthfully live in that property.

Then the question is, what's "capital property"?

It's also helpful to look at the other side of capital, that is "business property", can sometimes be referred to as inventory.

Business is income. All profits you made from the sale of the property is considered income. A good example is flipping houses.

Capital property, in the context of residential real estate, can be your long-term buy and hold. Profits from the sale of this long-term buy and hold are considered capital gain. Only 50% of capital gain is taxable.

Capital property, if you reside in it, you are eligible to claim principal residence exemption on the profit and hence shelter a portion or all of the gain. No tax liability.

CRA uses a set of criteria to determine whether a property is capital property or business.

They look at the taxpayer's course of the conduct. So if a taxpayer moves into a new home, renovates it, sells it, and does so repeatedly, CRA may take the position that this does not qualify for capital property.

Not a capital property, no principal residence exemption.

The profits on the sale are treated as income. Ouch!

They also look at whether the taxpayer has insider knowledge of the real estate market.

CRA had taken the position anyone that had any type of profession related to the real estate is considered to have special knowledge of the real estate market.

From real estate agents, mortgage agents, real estate lawyers, to as far fetch as an engineer working in the construction industry.

If you have insider knowledge, the transaction is more likely to be considered as income account, not capital. Ouch!

Again, 100% taxable, no principal residence exemption.

They also look at the taxpayer's primary and secondary intention.

As I often said in my presentation, problem is, intention is subjective.

How do you prove your intention at the time?

A taxpayer's intention was always to move into the property and stay there for a long time.

Circumstances change and sometimes we have to move on. That's called life.

In recent cases, CRA would take the purchase of 2nd property (after the sale of the 1st home) to prove that the 1st sale was intended to be trading property.

1st sale was ruled as business income and no principal residence exemption was allowed. Ouch!

With new homes, CRA took the position to go after taxpayers who did not reside in the homes for more than one year.

The truth is, the law does not require the taxpayer to live in the property for more than one year to claim it as principal residence.

The test for principal residence is whether a taxpayer "ordinarily inhabits" the property.

CRA also does not take into consideration the occupancy period (the period that allows the owners to move in but property has not closed yet).

If you purchase a new condo, move in during occupancy period for 7 months, live there for another 8 months and sell it, CRA may still be going after you even though you've lived in the property for over 12 months.

If you purchase a new house with the intention to move in, but life circumstances change and you did not move in, you also

can't claim that new house as your principal residence.
Intention does not matter in the context of principal residence.

What if you truthfully lived in the property, you realized that the place was way too small for your growing family and moved out? And you needed the money from the sale to purchase your second home?

In this case, documentation matters to prove that you "ordinarily inhabits" this property.

Change addresses for all government related matters – driver license, tax returns address, OHIP, etc.

Life pictures can also be useful to defend yourself that you truthfully live in the place. Pictures of birthday parties, Halloween parties, Christmas parties, etc. can also be evidence that you lived there.

Oh yes, email correspondence among your friends to plan the parties can also substantiate your claim!

Renting out a basement or using a portion of home as business

As real estate investors, I would assume the majority of us have read the book *Rich Dad Poor Dad* written by Robert Kiyosaki. It was the book that changed my life and my perspective on money.

Being a Chartered Accountant, I was blessed to make a decent living right out of university. From my early days as a co-op student to a full time position, I had never needed to worry about getting a job with decent pay.

Thanks to my parents, I was debt free since I graduated. Being able to make a decent living with limited expense early on helped me with the purchase of my first residence – a condo in Richmond Hill. From there on, as I progressed through the corporate ladder, I made more money. I got a nicer car and a bigger home. I was the classic 'middle class' described in *Rich Dad Poor Dad*. This was when the problem came in. I started noticing that I had no money in my bank account. I lived pay cheque to pay cheque.

Robert Kiyosaki said that, "assets produce income whether you work or not." It was then I realized, my nice car was a liability, my executive Toronto townhouse was also a liability!

None of these assets are producing ANY income for me.

It took me a while to make changes in life. We refinanced the townhouse to purchase our first student rental. We have also rented out the townhouse for a great rental return. And, we live in a detached home with a walkout basement, which is currently rented out to a tenant.

We turned the majority of these liabilities into money producing assets.

Many investors, who are like us, have rented out their basement to generate extra income.

That got the accountant in me to start thinking, *"Would that affect the status of principal residence exemption in Canada Revenue Agency's eyes?"*

For a property to qualify as principal residence (and hence the gain on disposition is tax exempt), the taxpayer or taxpayer's family (spouse or child) must "ordinarily inhabit" in this particular property. A family unit can only claim one property as the principal residence in any given year.

If you live in the house and you rent out your basement, this is considered a partial change in use in CRA's eyes. If you have undergone a structural change to section off the space for income producing purpose, the Income Tax Act provides for a deemed disposition of this converted portion of the house. The gain on the deemed disposition is being sheltered by the principal residence exemption. No tax would need to be paid on it.

You can deduct capital cost allowance (CCA) on the capital cost of that portion of the house, and any cost involved in altering the house against the rental income.

At the same time, you are also required to pay tax on the capital gain you earned on this converted portion, so NO principal residence exemption!

What's considered "structural change" is more substantial and permanent in nature. Examples include conversion on front half of the house into a store, conversion of a house into a self-contained domestic establishment for earning rental income (a duplex or triplex).

However, CRA's policy is not to apply this deemed disposition rule provided that the following criteria is met:

1. The income producing use is ancillary to the main use of the property as a residence
2. There is no structural change to the property; and
3. No CCA is claimed on the property

In our case, we did not do any alteration structurally (we bought the house that has a secondary suite) and hence no structural change was made. Although it was producing good income monthly, it is only sufficient to cover our monthly maintenance cost and we, as a family, are still occupying the major section of the house. The income producing use is therefore considered ancillary to our residence use. And of course, we will not claim any CCA at all, just so that we can preserve the principal residence status on this house!

Luckily, in our case, the deemed disposition rule does not apply to us. Converting liability into income producing asset is great, but make sure you do it in the most tax efficient manner.

Cottage

For those of you who own a lovely cottage as your secondary home, do you know the tax implications it has when you sell it?

Because you live in the cottage for a part of the year, Income Tax Act actually allows you to designate your cottage as principal residence (PR).

Unfortunately, a taxpayer is only allowed to designate one place as their PR. If you're married or in a common law relationship, you and your spouse/partner are only allowed to designate ONE place as your PR.

A taxpayer is only allowed to designate one place as their PR in a particular year.

The Income Tax Act uses the following formula to calculate the PR exemption:

(# of years home is PR + 1) x capital gain
# of years home is owned

Say you purchased your cottage in 2001 for $200K and you just sold it in 2015 for $450K. You got your own home since 2000 for $350K and the house is now worth $750K.

So, how do you decide which house to designate as PR?

The average annual gain on your cottage is ($450K – $200K)/(2015-2001+1) = $16,667 per year.

The expected average annual gain on your home is ($750K – $350K)/(2015-2000+1) = $25,000 per year.

In theory, the math is simple, you should designate your home as your PR in all the years since your average annual gain is higher with your home.

But the taxpayer can use the formula to their advantage to shelter a portion of the gain you make on selling the cottage. Let's revisit the formula again!

(# of years home is PR + 1) x capital gain
# of years home is owned

Canada Revenue Agency (CRA) recognizes that a taxpayer may buy and sell a place in the same year and hence own two places in the same year, therefore, they inserted the "+1" in the formula to allow a taxpayer to fully shelter two houses as their principal residence.

And because of the "+1" in the formula, a taxpayer can designate one year less in their home and still fully shelter the capital gain.

Using the example above, the taxpayer would designate his home from year 2000 to 2014 as the PR, and designate the cottage as his PR for year 2015.

Using the formula, PR exemption for his own home, # of years home is PR = 15 years, # of years home is owned = 16

| (15 + 1) x ($750K – $350K) / 16 | = $400K (the entire gain is exempted!) |

PR exemption for his cottage is then calculated as follow:

| (1 + 1) x ($450K – $200K) / 15 | = $33,333 (Two years of gain is exempted!) |

And the taxpayer will only pay tax on $450,000 – $200,000 – $33,333 = $216,667, instead of the full $350,000 gain.

You may wonder what happen if your home value in the future drops and your average annual gain goes below $16,667 per year when you actually sell your home. Unfortunately this is a risk that the taxpayer has to decide to take. There is always a risk for you to designate your current home as your principal residence and not maximize the principal residence exemption benefit. Be sure to discuss this with us when the issue comes up.

The calculation can get complicated and technical. Make sure you speak to us when you decide to sell your cottage. Be sure to understand the tax impact on the sale before you proceed.

Cherry Chan, CPA, CA

Little known 4 year extension on principal residence

My brother in law, Tony, who has recently become a real estate investor. He's in the process of turning his principal residence into a rental property and planning to rent afterwards.

Most real estate investors are aware that we do not need to pay tax on the capital gain incurred on our principal residence. But what happens if you move out from your current residence and turn it into a rental property?

In the eyes of the Income Tax Act, you have disposed your home at fair market value at the time. Because you have been living at the house, you can designate the house as your principal residence and thus shelter all the capital gain you have made.

Of course, you need to get some support for the fair market value of the property. An independent appraisal is often advised, and it should be done at the time of the change of use.

With the new rules imposed in 2016, you are now also required to report the change of use on your personal tax return when you are converting a primary residence into a rental property.

Now, back to Tony, since he is renting his next home, few people know that Income Tax Act actually allows him to continue to designate this property as principal residence for four more years, provided that he does not designate any other properties for the same period.

So say Tony purchased the property for $300,000 in 2008. The property is now worth $500,000 in 2015. A deemed disposition would have occurred for him in 2015 sheltering the $200,000 as part of the principal residence exemption.

Keeping our fingers crossed, this property will be worth $650,000 in 2019. With this election, he can shelter another $150,000 capital gain!

An election has to be filed at the same time with Canada Revenue Agency.

During this four-year extension, Tony cannot claim capital cost allowance on the building to offset the rental income he earns on this property.

In addition to this election, Canada Revenue Agency even allows a taxpayer to extends the principal residence exemption indefinitely if the following conditions are met:

- The taxpayer lives away from the principal residence because his employer would want him to relocate
- The taxpayer and the employer are unrelated
- The taxpayer returns to the original home after the employment is terminated
- And the temporary residence is at least 40km away from the original home

When you do decide to make your next big move, make sure you educate yourself and maximize the principal residence exemption.

Cherry Chan, CPA, CA

Preserving interest deductibility when converting Principal Residence to a rental property

We recently visited an old friend who lives in Unionville, Markham.

Unionville is a nice area, with many little boutique shops.

It is also the area where one of the best high schools in Ontario is located.

As most real estate investors know, great schools always increase the housing price nearby.

Our friends mentioned that they would like to trade their twenty year old home for a brand new modern looking home in Aurora eventually.

What if they don't trade homes? What if they simply refinance their current home, pull out the equity, purchase their new home with this equity and turn this one into a rental?

Of course, we learned from above that the interest incurred on money borrowed to earn investment is deductible and interest incurred on money borrowed to finance your own home is <u>not</u> deductible.

Savvy real estate investors like you and I may ask – is there a way to make the interest deductible?

I stumbled across this strategy last week.

The individuals would first sell their home to a corporation.

The corporation then issues a promissory note to the individuals.

Then the corporation would apply for a regular mortgage to finance this house. And use the proceeds to repay the individuals.

Therefore the entire mortgage interest on the presumably 80% loan to value of this house is deductible. Smart, eh?

The individuals can then use the money to purchase their new dream home.

One of the biggest disadvantages is that the couple would have to pay the land transfer tax.

When the individuals sell their home to the corporation, land transfer tax is triggered, calculated based on the fair market value of the house at the time the transaction occurred.

For our friends, their house is currently worth $1.4million. Land transfer tax will cost roughly $24,475.

That's a lot of $$$ to begin with.

Of course, for taxpayers who live in Toronto, the land transfer tax can be doubled.

Definitely you need to look at whether the tax deduction on the interest is worthwhile making you pay the land transfer tax.

This couple paid $800,000 for the house a few years back. If their current mortgage balance is $500,000.

By refinancing the house to 80% loan to value, the couple can take out $620,000 to purchase their next home. Wow!

Let's work out the numbers.

If they can borrow up to 80% loan to value ($1,120,000) in their old residence, the interest cost (with 2.5% interest rate) for the first five years is $131,268. Roughly $470K interest cost for the entire term.

We learn from the previous blog post that only the portion related to the rental would be deductible. In this case, only interest related to the $500,000 of $1,120,000 is deductible.

For the first five years, $58,602 is deductible and $72,666 is not deductible.

For the entire mortgage term (25 years), $210K is deductible and $260K is not deductible as a result.

Depending on how much money you make personally – if you are a high income earner, the tax cost is roughly 50% of the non-deductible portion.

If you don't plan on selling the first home in five years, the tax cost for not deducting the interest is $31,333. If you don't plan on selling the first home forever, the tax cost is $130K.

Now compared to the land transfer tax you will have to pay to sell it to a corporation of $24K, it doesn't sound too bad all of a sudden.

If you already have a corporation or small business to begin with, this strategy can be a better one.

Special cases

Rent to own taxation

This year marks the 15th anniversary of my time spent living in Canada. I wake up every morning feeling grateful to live here in an established economy with freedom.

Thinking back home to Hong Kong, where the housing market is so outrageous, I would not be able to afford a property to live in.

Let alone have the opportunity to invest in properties, like I do here in Canada.

In fact, I would have made a good candidate for a rent-to-own program back in Hong Kong.

But thankfully things are different here in Canada.

As Canadian real estate investors, we get the privilege to help other Canadians find an affordable and manageable means to home ownership.

In a typical rent-to-own situation, there is usually two parties involved; the investor or landlord, and the tenant/buyer. Usually the buyer doesn't have enough money for a downpayment or high enough credit score to finance the purchase of a home.

This is why the buyer enters into an agreement with the landlord with the option to own the property at the end of the program. Most agreements are within 2-3 years but they can be longer, and at the end, the property is purchased at a pre-specified price while the tenant lives in it.

This is why they're referred to as tenant/buyers.

Rent-to-own programs make for a great investment because there are 3 streams of income for the investor to profit from:

1. The tenant/buyer is required to give a downpayment to obtain the right to purchase the home. The downpayment will be offset against the purchase price when the tenant/buyer exercises the option.

2. On a monthly basis, the tenant pays the investor/landlord rent, plus an additional amount that goes towards the purchase price of the property at the end of the program.

3. By the end of the 2-3 year period, if the tenant/buyer's credit score is good enough to qualify for a mortgage and decides to exercise the option to purchase the home, the landlord receives the pre-specified purchase price, less any of the downpayment and monthly amounts received over the course of the rental period.

These are the 3 streams of *passive income* an investor can receive from a rent-to-own program.

You can probably see how such agreements can benefit both parties. the tenant/buyer gets to purchase the property at the end of the rental period and achieve their goal of home ownership, while the investor profits from 3 streams of income.

Rent-to-own programs are just another example of the opportunities available to people and families living in Canada and why this is such a great country to call home.

Complete Taxation Guide to Canadian Real Estate Investing

There are 3 streams of income an investor can acquire when investing in rent to own. And how you would report those incomes depends on the landlord's personal circumstances.

Firstly, we must determine if the landlord is operating this rent-to-own as an investment or as a business.

If the rent-to-own transaction is considered as a business, the 3 streams of income are all required to be reported as income.

The Canada Revenue Agency (CRA) uses the following factors to determine whether the rent-to-own transaction is capital in nature (an investment) or a business.

1. Is the rent to own transaction similar to the landlord's *normal course of business*?
    - If the landlord is a full-time landlord that does not have any other employment income, the rent-to-own transaction is more likely to be treated as the landlord's normal course of business.
    - On the other hand, if the landlord has a full-time job, it is more difficult to CRA to argue that the rent-to-own is similar to the landlord's normal course of business. *Be cautioned that one single factor cannot be relied upon to conclude that the rent-to-own transaction is not considered as a business.
2. How frequently does the landlord invest in rent-to-own deals?
    - The more rent-to-own deals the landlord has, the more likely that CRA considers it as business.
3. Is this rent-to-own transaction an *adventure or concern in the nature of trade*?
    - An adventure or concern in the nature of trade is something a landlord habitually does that is capable

of producing a profit, irrespective of the landlord's own occupation.

- There are 3 factors that the CRA will consider the rent-to-own transaction as an adventure or concern in the nature of trade:

    1. Whether the landlord dealt with the property acquired by him in the same way as a dealer in such property?

        - We need to compare the landlord's conduct with that of what a dealer's conduct would be for the rent-to-own deals. The following factors are usually considered to determine whether the landlord's conduct consistent with a dealer's conduct:

            - If there is evidence of effort, such as advertising, were soon made to find or attract purchasers or that a sale took place within a short period of time, it is more likely CRA considers the landlord as a dealer.
            - The more renovation or extra steps that the landlord does to increase the marketability of the rent-to-own property, the more likely CRA considers him as a dealer.
            - If the landlord is a real estate agent or mortgage agent that has a commercial background in a similar business, the more likely CRA considers him as a dealer.

2. Whether the nature and quantity of the property excludes the possibility of generating income from the property other than selling it.

- In the rent-to-own situation, the nature of the property allows the landlord to rent it out to the tenants and hence supporting the transaction as capital in nature (an investment).

3. Whether the landlord's intention is consistent with other evidence pointing to a trading motivation

- The landlord's intention to sell the property at a profit alone cannot be used by itself to determine whether he was involved in the adventure or concern in the nature of trade. If one of the other above factors clearly shows that the landlord is engaged in the adventure or concern in the nature of trade, his intention can be viewed as corroborative evidence.

- The investor's intention can change over the period of time and can have more than one intention. If the investor's intention is to hold the rent-to-own investment as an investment (capital in nature), CRA also looks at the secondary intention if the investor is unable to fulfill the first intention.

I know some of that "legal talk" can be confusing but you should now be able to tell if your rent-to-own transaction will be considered as an investment or as a business.

Like I mention above, if it is considered business in nature, the investor is required to report the downpayment as income the year he receives it. He is also required to report the rent, and the rent credit, as income the years he receives those.

Ultimately, he is also required to report the sale of the property, if the tenant chooses to exercise the option, as income the year the option agreement ends.

I am going to discuss the treatment of these 3 streams of income if the RTO arrangement is to be considered capital in nature.

1. Downpayment for the option to purchase the house at a specified price

Depending on how the arrangement has been written, if the non-refundable downpayment is used to pay for the option to purchase the house at the end of the 2 or 3 year term, the Income Tax Act (ITA) allows the taxpayer to report the downpayment as capital gain the year he receives the money.

If the agreement does not specify this amount is for the purpose of purchasing the option and because it is non-refundable, the investor is required to report it as income.

However, in most rent-to-own option agreements I've worked on it clearly specifies that the downpayment is used to pay for the option. It's most likely, the investor can report it as the capital gain in the year he receives it.

2. Monthly rent and the rent credit

For the monthly rent component, similar to any rental income, the investor has to report it as income the year he receives it.

As for the rent credit, the tax treatment depends on how your agreement is written.

If it is written in a way that the rent credit is used to maintain the option to purchase the house at the end of the 2 or 3 year term, similar to the downpayment, the rent credit can then be reported as capital gain the year the investor receives it.

I had a discussion with some rent-to-own experts about this rent credit reporting treatment. One concern that was raised was if the agreements clearly specified the rent credit is for the maintenance of the purchasing option at the end, such agreement may not be able to stand the ruling at the Landlord Tenant Board in case the tenant/buyer defaults their rent.

Most importantly, the amount of rent credit collected on an annual basis is small. The corresponding tax liability is also low in comparison.

3. Purchase option at the end

If the tenant/buyer does not exercise the option at the end of the 2 or 3 year term, and all the reporting has been done properly then the landlord investor has nothing to worry about.

If the tenant/buyer exercises the option at the end of the option period, the landlord investor must take the following steps:

> 1. For the years that the landlord investor reports capital gain on the downpayment and rent credit, amended return needs to be filed to reduce the capital gain.
> 2. For the current year, the landlord investor adds the downpayment and the rent credit (received in prior years) to the proceeds and reports the cost of the house accordingly to calculate the capital gain.

And that's it!

That's really all you need to know about Rent-to-Own taxation. You should now be able to tell if your RTO arrangement is a business or capital in nature, and know how to report the 3 streams of income you receive during the RTO period when you have to file your taxes.

Buying and selling new built

I love the convenience of living in a condo. It's cozy and convenient. And I don't have to care about pipe burst if I go on a vacation!

Many people also prefer condo living partly because of the convenience that it offers and partly because of the affordability.

Others, real estate investors specifically, prefer new built for the fact that they don't have to do as much repairs and there's an accrued accumulation of value from the date of purchase to the date of closing. They can easily liquidate it before or after closing and make some fantastic profit off the transactions.

New construction homes can take a couple of years to complete. Some can be as long as five to six years to build.

When the taxpayer decides to purchase the condo unit 5 years ago, his plan was to move in and enjoy his single life.

Life changes in these 5 years. He met a girl and started a family with a kid. The original one bedroom condo is no longer perfect for his family.

Now at closing, he doesn't need the property anymore. He can either rent it out or sell it. The tax impact depends on the transaction.

Whether he sells it or rents it out, he will likely receive a letter from CRA asking for his HST rebate back. See the discussion in next section.

If he rents it out, rental income less all allowable deductions is reported as ordinary income.

If he chooses to sell it immediately, the sale can be treated as income by CRA and 100% is taxable.

Wait a minute, it was intended for his principal residence. Can't he simply claim principal residence exemption on it?

Unfortunately, the first criteria to claim principal residence exemption on a property is that the taxpayer must ordinarily inhabit at the property.

If he sells it before closing, it's called assignment of sale. He's never lived in the property.

If he sells it shortly after closing, he also doesn't live in the property and still does not qualify him to claim principal residence exemption unfortunately.

Well, sophisticated taxpayers may then ask, can't he report it as capital gain, which is only 50% taxable? Income is 100% taxable.

If we go through the criteria to determine whether such a transaction should be considered capital or income:

i. *The nature of the property sold;*

   The unit sold was a condo for residential use.

ii. *The length of time the taxpayer was in possession as owner of the property;*

Complete Taxation Guide to Canadian Real Estate Investing

The condo was in possession for a short period of time, two months, before it was sold.

Note that CRA currently does not take into account the duration of occupancy period (the period which a taxpayer can use the property but does not truly own the property yet).

He may have an occupancy period of 10 months before he sells it in 2 months after closing. He can be living there for the first 10 months but he still can't claim the property as principal residence if he did not live in there for the 2 months after legal ownership transferred.

iii. *The frequency and number of operations carried out by the taxpayer;*

In this particular example, we make the assumption that this is the only new condo he sold. He does not own any other things.

iv. *The improvements made by the taxpayer to the property;*

The taxpayer likely didn't do any improvement given that the condo is brand new.

v. *The circumstances surrounding the sale of the property; and*
Say the taxpayer needs to some cash to finish the purchase of his family home.
He's also an accountant, not a real estate accountant, does not work in the real estate industry.

vi. *The taxpayer's intention at the time the property was acquired, as indicated by the taxpayer's actions.*

Intention is subjective. How do you prove your intention when it was 5 years ago?

It's tough to prove anything you did five years ago, let alone your intention.

CRA would take the position that the taxpayer's intention was to sell, given that it was sold shortly after closing in 2 months.

It becomes a he said she said situation.

[11] In addition to these criteria, Canadian courts have developed the "secondary intention" criterion that may apply even when the taxpayer's main intention has been established as making a long-term investment. This criterion applies if, at the time the property was acquired, the taxpayer had considered the possibility of selling the property for a profit if the long-term investment project could not be achieved for whatever reason."[4]

Secondary intention is a tough one. Secondary intention is almost similar to "what's the worst case scenario if I don't move in".

---

[4] http://decision.tcc-cci.gc.ca/tcc-cci/decisions/en/29747/1/document.do

If the taxpayer's secondary intention was to sell if he couldn't move in at that time, that's sufficient to support CRA's position that such transaction should be treated as income.

The line isn't clear on all these.

Based on the analysis above, I would definitely claim this transaction on capital account. Keep in mind that you can still be audited and CRA may not agree with this analysis. They may take a stronger position that you always intended to sell.

Your responsibility is to gather as much information as possible to prove your position.

HST on new builts

Many investors and clients prefer buying brand new houses for obvious reasons. Out of the stack of legal documents the buyers are asked to sign, one of them is a declaration that the buyers or the buyers' relatives are moving into the property. This allows the buyers to assign the right to claim HST rebate to the builders.

Many people are unaware that the builders' posted sale price already accounted for the New Housing Rebate. Let's illustrate using an example.

Purchase price before HST = $300,000

HST at 13% = $300,000 × 13% = $39,000 (Federal portion = $39,000 × 5 ÷ 13 = $15,000; Ontario portion = $39,000 × 8 ÷ 13 = $24,000)

HST rebate Federal Portion = $15,000 × 36% (up to maximum of $6,300) = $5,400

HST rebate Ontario Portion = $24,000 × 75% (up to a maximum of $24,000) = $18,000

Builders' advertised price is usually = $300,000 + $39,000 − $5,400 − $18,000 = $315,600

In most cases, the builders take on the responsibility to claim the HST rebate. Canada Revenue Agency (CRA) allows the builders to claim the HST rebate back on behalf of the property owners provided that the property owners are moving into the newly constructed properties.

As a result, out of the hundreds of pages of documents you are required to sign when you purchase a new home, there is a document relating to you declaring that you are going to move into the property.

What if you clearly know that you are buying for the purpose of investing?

CRA also offers the same amount of HST rebate called GST/HST New Residential Rental Property Rebate. The only difference between this rebate and the New Housing Rebate is that the investors are not allowed to assign the right to the builders to claim the HST rebate on behalf of them.

In another words, when the deal is closed, the investor has to pay the builder the purchase price plus the full HST. In the example above, it is $300,000 + 39,000 = $339,000 instead of $315,600.

The GST/HST New Residential Rental Property Rebate allows the investors to apply for the HST rebate, same amount as the one available under the New Housing Rebate, provided that you have a one year lease agreement signed.

In our example, the same amount of $5,400 Federal rebate and $18,000 Ontario rebate are refundable provided that you have a one year lease agreement signed.

You can follow the instructions in this link to file your application form accordingly. http://www.cra-arc.gc.ca/E/pbg/gf/gst524/README.html

Once you fill out the form, you are required to attach a copy of the lease agreement, a copy of the statement of adjustments, the agreement of purchase and sale together with the application form and submit it to the government.

Cherry Chan, CPA, CA

My experience with the process is that it would take about 2 to 3 months turnaround time and the government will send you the money directly.

What if you are planning to flip the new property only?

There is much media coverage about the CRA going after taxpayers who claim to move into the newly constructed house but didn't. They assigned the rebate to the builder but sold the investment properties before or shortly after closing.

Unfortunately, the taxpayers are then liable to repay the CRA for the HST rebate and they are not eligible to claim the GST/HST New Residential Rental Property Rebate.

As a result of recent media coverage and also the fact that many people are found not complying with the law, CRA has been focusing their auditing effort in the real estate related activities.

Between April 2015 and September 2016, CRA had completed over 13 thousands audits in Ontario alone.

Close to 11 thousands of these audit cases are specifically related to the GST/HST New Housing and New Residential Rental Property Rebates.

They recovered $210 million in total, $144 million was related to the HST New Housing and New Residential Rental Property Rebates.

The amount recovered in BC is substantially lower.

GST/HST New Residential Rental Property Rebates are the low hanging fruit.

I discussed in my previous blog post how the rebates work.

Complete Taxation Guide to Canadian Real Estate Investing

There are two types of rebates, one is the New Residential Housing Rebates (Housing Rebates) and the other one is the New Residential Rental Property Rebates (Rental Rebates).

Generally speaking, if you intend to move into the property at the time when you sign the agreement of purchase and sale, you are qualified to claim the Housing Rebates.

For many people, you claim the Housing Rebates through your builder, as you are eligible to assign the right to the builder to claim it on behalf of you.

This essentially lowers your purchase price by the Housing Rebates amount.

The problem is, more often than not, that new builds are delayed. It can take 4 to 5 years before you can close the property in your name.

More often than not, circumstances change and the newly built is not longer a perfect fit to the buyer's personal situation.

He may move in for a while and realize that the new place doesn't work for him anymore. Or he can choose to sell it immediately (before or shortly after closing). He can also choose to rent it out.

Many taxpayers then get hit by a tax bill asking them for the Housing Rebates back. This can be as high as $30K.

Housing Rebates are different from Principal Residence Exemption. You qualify to claim Housing Rebates if you intend to move into the property at the time the agreement of purchase and sale is signed.
Intention is tricky though. How do you prove your intention?

This is not meant to be an exhaustive list, but do make sure that you keep all the hydro bills, all government records address updated, kids parties, emails, any documentation that can prove that your intention was to move into the place.

What if you and your wife are both on title?

In one of the cases discussed in the course, both husband and wife were purchasing the condo together. One spouse lives in it only during the weekend while stays at a different location for work during the week.

CRA took the position that only 50% of the HST Housing Rebate was allowed and disallowed the other 50% of the HST.

CRA was not correct. The couple took the case to court and subsequently won.

But that's CRA's position!

What if you and a few unrelated friends bought a new built together?

Everyone has to intend to live in this new built as the primary place of residence.

If you and three other friends bought a one bedroom condo and declared that the intention was to move in and claimed the HST Housing Rebate, that's probably not going to fly.

Only the person who lived in the property would be qualified to claim the HST Housing Rebate and ONLY that portion of it

could be claimed.

Wow! That's tough!

On the other hand, if you and the other three friends bought a new four bedroom house together and intended to reside at the property, you may be qualified to claim the full HST Housing Rebate.

Now say circumstances change, friendship broke down and you guys decided not to live together anymore before the new built is completed.

You sell the new built on assignment.

You now have to pay HST on the assignment fees! Yes, it is a taxable supply under the Excise Tax Act.

CRA took the position that the portion related to the deposit paid to the builder would still be subject to HST, but one subsequent court case had concluded otherwise. So no HST on the deposit portion.

What if you are the buyer of this assignment? Can you still qualify for the HST rebate?

Typically speaking, when you purchase an assignment of new built, the lawyer usually prepared the direction of title change and that's the end of the story.

CRA seems to be taking the position that it is not sufficient enough because the buyer did not absorb all liabilities from the initial seller.

It is unclear at this moment whether a direction of title change is sufficient to qualify the assignee (the buyer of the assignment contract) to claim the HST Housing Rebate, provided that he is intending to move into the property.

If I were to purchase an assignment deal, I would definitely consult a lawyer to make sure the proper documentation is done.

Say if the assignee also paid HST on assignment, he's essentially paying HST on the assignment AND the HST on the new built, two taxable supplies.

Depending on the purchase price, provided that you intend to move into the property, it may be worthwhile NOT to assign the right to the builder to claim it on behalf of you.

Instead, you put in the form to claim it yourself so that you can include the HST paid on both assignment fees and the new built.

That's it about the HST Housing Rebates & HST Rental Property Rebates.

Right or Wrong Things to Do Paying Your Contractors Cash

A few of my clients asked me recently whether they should take a cash deal offered by the contractors when they renovate their rental properties.

As a licensed accountant, it's my responsibility to advise you that you should not engage in any underground transactions.

I am a number person. Let's analyze it from the number perspective.

Usually, when we are offered a cash deal, we don't have to pay for the HST.

For a $20,000 project, HST 13% is equivalent to $2,600, total project price is $22,600.

If the taxpayer pays cash, he's got a cash deal of $20K.

If the taxpayer owns the property in his own name and assume that his marginal tax rate is 40%, the renovation of $22,600 is equivalent to $9,040 tax savings. (For simplicity's sake, let's assume that the entire $20,000 is repairs and can be deducted as a current expense.)

The true after tax cost is $22,600 − $9,040 = $13,560.

If the taxpayer were to pay cash, he cannot deduct the expense he incurred.

Hence, he is using after tax money to finance the renovation, which means the after tax cost is $20,000.

Now, if the taxpayer owns the property in the corporation, and assuming the property is a regular rental property, the passive income is taxed at 50%. Therefore, the after tax cost of paying the full price for the renovation is only $11,200 ($22,600 x 50%).

As you can see, it is almost always better to do it the right way. The taxpayer is almost always in the worse end of the deal.

So, when you are negotiating with the contractor next time, make sure you are doing so above the board, get the proper receipt and get the full deduction.

Guide to AirBnB taxation

Last week I finally found a place in Florida to stay for our February trip.

Last year, we planned a cruise trip. Like all the cruise trips we had been on, we booked an early flight to Fort Lauderdale the day the cruise set sail.

I am a BIG cruise lover. I've been on over 15 cruises myself and I had never once missed the boat.

Turned out the Pearson airport ground staff were mostly sick that day and our flight got delayed for 4 hours before leaving Toronto. We took off at the time when we were supposed to arrive in Fort Lauderdale.

We ended up missing our ship. We could catch the boat in its next stop in Mexico but we had to take two connecting flights, over 10 hours of travel to get there. Erwin and I just decided to stay in Fort Lauderdale with Robin. We stayed in a hotel by the beach for a week and we still had an amazing time altogether.

This time around it's more complicated. Instead of traveling with one kid, we have two now. My mom and my brother are visiting from Hong Kong. My aunt and my cousin are also joining us. It's their first cruise trip.

We have a big group this time and simply can't afford any problems. We can't take the risk of missing the boat.

So we decided to go to Miami a few days before. This gives them the opportunity to tour the city and it guarantees that we will be able to catch the ship!

As you can imagine, it can be quite expensive to find a hotel that will accommodate us all. And because of the kids, it's actually better to stay at a place that has a kitchen.

Like most people do, we turned to the biggest hotel chain in the world that does not own any hotels – AirBnB.ca!

Through the website, I was able to find places available that could accommodate all eight of us and fit our budget.

Based on the customer reviews, I was able to find a place in a good neighborhood relatively quickly.

Undoubtedly, AirBnB home sharing has become a very popular way of accommodation.

For the real estate investors locally who want to operate an AirBnB accommodation, what is the tax implication of this?

As a Canadian tax resident, you are required by law to report your worldwide income, whether you earn it legally or illegally.

So if you operate an AirBnB on your vacation home in Florida, you are still required to report the income on your Canadian tax return.

If you operate an AirBnB in your Canadian properties, AirBnB leaves the tax filing responsibility to the Canadian home owners.

You are responsible to keep track of all the income you generate from operating these short term rentals and report them on your tax returns.

Similar to all rental properties, any expenses you incur for the purpose of earning the rental income are deductible.

Complete Taxation Guide to Canadian Real Estate Investing

The 3% host service fees being charged by AirBnB is a deductible expense against your rental income.

Cleaner's fees are deductible, alongside with utilities, repairs & maintenance, condo fees, mortgage interest, etc.

This place I am staying has three bedrooms with three queen sized beds, a fully equipped kitchen with all appliances.

These furniture and appliances can be capitalized and capital cost allowance (depreciation) can be taken on these assets accordingly to offset against your income. Care should be taken into differentiating between a capital asset and regular repairs and maintenance cost.

Now if you rent out only a portion of your home to the AirBnB travelers, and you still live in the house, you need to be extremely careful with the portion of expenses that you are deducting.

You are only allowed to deduct the portion of expenses that are related to the AirBnB rental business. Say 40% of your house is rented to the AirBnB travelers, only 40% of mortgage interest, utilities, property taxes, insurance, repairs & maintenance, etc. are deductible against the income.

If you rent out more than 50% of your home as AirBnB, you may no longer be able to claim principal residence exemption on this house. (To qualify to claim the principal residence exemption, the rental portion must be ancillary to you living there. Also, no capital cost allowance can be taken on the building cost.)

You may also run into the HST issue if you make more than $30K a year. Generally speaking, residential property rentals are HST exempt. CRA may argue that the AirBnB hosts are operating the place on commercial terms, similar to what hotel operations would be and hence your rental income could be subject to HST.

The responsibility is on the hosts to setup the charge of HST or else you are responsible to pay for the HST yourself.

AirBnB is a great platform for home sharing. Although there is a lot of management involved, the money you can get from these short-term rentals can be quite substantial.

Be aware of these tax implications when you choose to operate a home sharing business!

For now, I am just happy that we found a beautiful place to stay in Florida.

Joint Venture Accounting

I was the classic middle class when I worked for the largest retail store in Canada.

For those of you who had read the book Rich Dad Poor Dad written by Robert Kiyosaki, you would know what I am talking about.

Yep. I made decent money, but I spent every penny of it. I lived pay check by pay check.

I drove a Mercedes that I didn't need and I lived in a big townhouse that had more washrooms than I needed.

I justified the spending by betting that I would only get raises in the future, not the other way around.

I never put much thought into investing in real estate, after all, I lived pay check by pay check. All I could afford was the big executive townhouse that I was in.

I'd had the book Rich Dad Poor Dad for the longest time sitting on the shelf but I never bothered to read it.

Not until I met my husband Erwin. (He's Mr Hamilton, specialized working with real estate investors who invest in Hamilton and the surrounding area.)

He was mortgage free before he was 30. He got a few houses under his belt at the time. He carried this sense of pride about his investments that I've never seen anyone around me having.

But I was practically broke. I made more money than he did but I was practically broke.

He drove a beat-up Honda Accord at the time and I drove a brand-new Mercedes. That could be the difference.

I started looking for answer, hoping to find it in Rich Dad Poor Dad.

Reading this book was a life changing moment in my life. I realized what I owned, both the Mercedes and the Executive Townhome were really a liability to me, not an asset.

I really should invest in something that can generate income whether I work or not.

The fact that I was dating Mr Hamilton at the time made me realize, for the first time, that I could purchase a property outside of Toronto for a fraction of what I paid for my townhouse.

We started talking about refinancing my executive townhouse (finally turning it into an asset) and taking out the equity to purchase my first investment property.

I'd only dated him for 6 months at the time. He found the property in St Catharines on the most desirable student rental street. He went out and did all the leg work.

All I did was sitting at my corporate job signing paperwork to qualify for financing. I didn't even see the property before closing.

That was my first joint venture deal.

Erwin was the real estate expert and I was the money partner.

I qualified for financing and pay for the downpayment and closing cost. He went out to do all the research, spoke to a couple of experts in the neighborhood who had done many student rentals, he got an engineer to inspect the house, found the contractor and did most of the upfront work.

I never really put much thought about my risk at the time. I was comfortable with the arrangement even though I've had only been with him for 6 months. After all, I was the one on title.

If our relationship doesn't work out, I would still be the one on title. Not sure if I would choose to give his 50% back to be honest, but hey, we're now married with two kids! ;)

We never went as far as formalizing our relationship to have a joint venture agreement at the time detailing the roles and responsibilities of each other and how the ownership structure would work.

Many people wonder what the proper tax impact is for a joint venture.

This really goes back the detail of your joint venture agreement between you and your partner. The terms and conditions, the financial risk and the income and expense split also drive how each partner should report the deal.

Complexity arises when the joint venture partners did not contribute the same amount of money and effort.

For the most part, joint venture taxation is based on what the underlying business is doing.

If the joint venture was formed to purchase a long-term buy and hold property, each joint venture partner owns 50% of income and expense and both partners are jointly liable for all the liabilities, chances are, you should report 50% of income and expenses and 50% of assets and liabilities.

What if the long-term buy and hold is a rent to own property? And the option downpayment received was given back to the money partner, should the real estate expert report the income the year they receive it, even though money wasn't really going into his pocket at all?

But if the JV agreement simply gives a guaranteed fixed rate of return to the money partner investor, such as an 8% return on the money he invests in, and upon sale of the property the money partner is also guaranteed an exact dollar return, one may argue that the money partner does not really own 50% of the property.

Joint venture can be quite complicated. Accounting and tax impact truly based on what the underlying agreement suggests.

But for us, Erwin and I reported our property truly 50/50 (to honour his effort that he put in)!

Corporations Talk

7 Questions to decide whether you should incorporate

Corporations provide a lot of flexibility in tax planning but the immediate cost to setup and maintain can sometimes be difficult to bear, especially for new investors who barely make any cash flow from the properties.

Whether you should incorporate seems to be the most asked questions among real estate investors. Unfortunately there is no one size fits all answer.

Here are the 7 questions I've come up with to help you prepare when making this difficult decision (PART 1).

1. Do you have a small business?

If you own a small business like I do and you don't need all the cash flow generated from the business to survive, you definitely should incorporate. Say a small business owner makes $150,000 net profit from his business before paying himself. If he pays himself full amount in salary, he nets about $103,000 in his pocket.

Now say he only really needs $60K after tax for his personal expense, he has $43K ($103K – $60K) left to be invested in his own personal name.

What if he doesn't take all the profit from the corporation?

He only needs to pay himself roughly $77K salary before tax to get to $60K after tax money for his personal expense.

This means that he has $73K profit ($150K – $77K) left in the corporation.

He needs to pay 15% tax on this $73K profit. And that is $11K.

After tax profit to invest in the corporation is $62,000.

So investing in a corporate structure means you have an extra $19K to invest! And this is only from one year!

If you own a small business and you do not need every dime from the business to live, you definitely should consider incorporating to invest faster.

2. Do you need the cash flow now?

Most accountants would argue that there are no benefits to owning the properties in the corporation. This is a very true statement.

There is something called tax integration in Canada.

Our tax system is designed in a way that you should end up with the same amount of money despite the ownership structure.

This means, you should be net more or less the same amount if you were to earn the rental income in your name vs earning it in a corporation and taking them out immediately.

If you need the cash flow from the properties immediately and declare the dividend to yourself the same year, chances are you are paying the same amount of taxes.

The accountants make the money by filing your taxes. Tax payers end up having less in their pocket.

Complete Taxation Guide to Canadian Real Estate Investing

Before you make the decision not to incorporate, you have to also consider other factors – such as the one after this.

3. Do you have someone to split income with? Real estate investing is considered a specified investment business in the eyes of Income Tax Act. What this means is that the net rental income you get from deducting all the eligible expenses are considered passive income. Passive income in a corporation is taxed at 50%.

That's a lot!

But out of this 50%, 30% is refundable when a taxable dividend is declared to the shareholder.

So you really only pay 20% (50% – 30%) over the long run in the corporation.

The key here is that you are declaring a taxable dividend to a shareholder.

So the shareholder has to report the income in his/her own name.

If this shareholder does not have any other income, you can pay minimal tax with the first $40,000 dividend.

Between the shareholder's personal tax rate at close to 0% and the 20% in the corporation, the combined tax rate is 20%.

When structure properly, corporation can lower your tax rate to as low as 20%! Isn't that amazing?

4. Are you concerned with legal liability protection? Admittedly I am not a lawyer and I am not the expert to discuss the legal liability protection that you get

from a corporation. A corporation is a separate legal entity in the eyes of the law. This means that it can be sued as a separate entity.
For any legal wrongdoing that the corporation may be a part of, it can stand in court by itself (to a certain extent).

Say you get sued by a tenant, the corporation can stand alone in court.

As an investor, I can tell you that the corporation can provide you a certain kind of legal protection.

But it's not everything.

For example, when we purchase the properties in the corporation's name, the bank often still requires the shareholders to guarantee the loan personally.

This means that if the corporation cannot afford to make the mortgage payment, the bank can still come after our personal assets.

5. **What are your long term goals? Are you planning to buy more than one property?**

As much flexibility as a corporation can give you, there is still an annual filing cost and initial setup cost that you have to invest in to get these benefits.As a real estate accountant, I often advise new investors to buy their first investment property in their personal names (unless they are doing flips).At the end of the day, how do you know if you are committed to invest in real estate long term?For some people, one is more than enough to handle.Setting up a corporation for simply one property is probably not worth it, unless it is a bigger project.Depending on the size of the investment and the projected income, one single family home inside one corporation may not be worth the benefit a corporation can provide.

On the other side, if you have a 75 unit apartment building, that can be a different story.

My advice? If your long term goal is to buy more than one property, then consider incorporating.

If this is your very first one and it is a single family rental,

don't worry about it.

6. **Are you planning to leave your assets to your kids?**

Corporation provides a lot of flexibility in terms of estate planning.For those of you who don't know, the tax man would still come after you for one final time at death.This means that you have to pay taxes on any capital gain you have accumulated on the assets you have owned.You would have deemed to dispose all the assets at the fair market value at death. Your children may not want to sell the properties at that time but they may not have a choice if you have accumulated significant amount of gain on them. Corporation allows some tax planning to be done. It can pass on the growth of the portfolio to future generations and limit the taxes at death.

It may even allow you to limit the probate taxes.

7. The cost of changing your mind can be costly!

It's expensive to change your mind. Many investors asked me if they would be allowed to transfer their properties over to the corporation at a later date when they do decide to incorporate.

The answer is always a yes, but it is just a matter of how much $$$ we are talking about.

For one, you will be incurring land transfer tax. In Ontario, if you sell your properties from yourself to your corporation, the ownership has changed and hence Ministry of Finance would charge you the Land Transfer Tax.

If your property is located in City of Toronto, the land transfer tax is doubled!

And that's just land transfer tax alone.

When you "transfer" the ownership of the property to the corporation, Canada Revenue Agency treats that as if a third party sale has occurred, unless you file a special election to defer the capital gain until the corporation sells the property to a third party.

This basically means:

- You pay taxes on the cumulative gain at the time of the transfer, which is dumb because there's essentially no change of ownership.
- You pay the accountant to file the election for you, which is generally from $1,000 and up.

If you look at the cost of changing your mind, comparing to the cost of simply setting up the corporation and paying for the filing fees for a couple of years, you may still be ahead by setting up the corporation early!

Incorporating or not is often a personal decision. Definitely consult an experienced real estate accountant to make sure you are maximizing your tax benefit.

Cherry Chan, CPA, CA

Examining the Pros & cons of 3 most common structures

Many investors have approached me in the last little while asking me when is the best time to incorporate to own real estate. Most people are often hesitant due to the initial setup costs and the annual filing costs involved in owning real estate in a corporation.

In my previous posts, I talked about my Big Why and how I plan to use corporations to achieve my Big Why in the most tax efficient manner.

In this post, I will briefly discuss and compare some common structures investors use, their benefits and pitfalls.

One corporation, multiple properties

Benefits

- Limited liability against personally owned assets
- Potential for income splitting opportunities

Complete Taxation Guide to Canadian Real Estate Investing

- Relatively low setup cost as only one corporation is used to own multiple properties
- If portfolio is large enough and investors hire more than five employees to manage the properties, rental income can be considered as active business income and enjoy 15.5% small business tax rate
- With proven record of financial performance from properties, potential for the bank to allow the corporation to qualify for financing on its own without personal guarantee on the mortgage

Pitfalls

- Annual filing cost is likely around $750 to $1,500 for one corporation; you need to make sufficient cash flow to cover the cost of annual filing.
- Rental income is considered passive income and hence is taxed at 46% in the corporation. If investor's marginal tax rate before rental income is less than 46%, no immediate tax savings
- Cannot prevent liability caused by landlord's gross negligence
- Personal guarantee on mortgage is likely required
- Qualification on mortgage can be more challenging with corporation

One corporation, one property

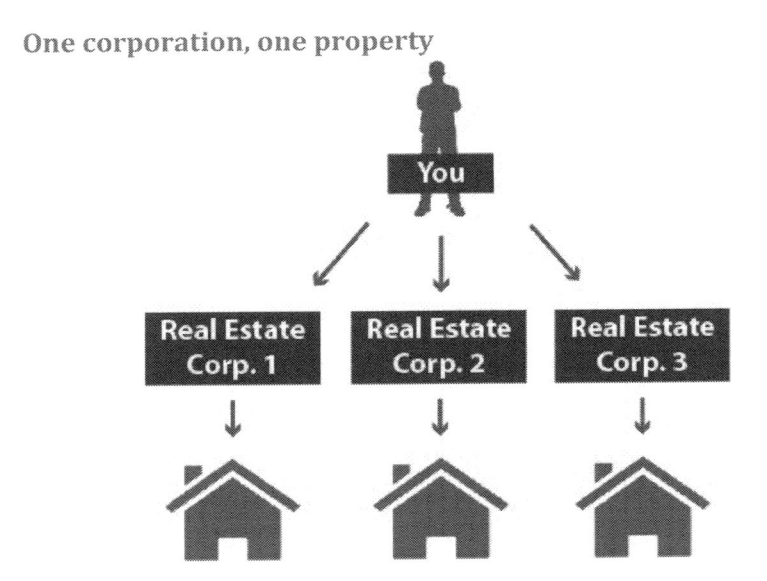

Benefits:

- Protection against principle residence from all rental properties
- Protection from one rental property against others
- Appropriate if rental portfolio is higher risk, such as large multi units buildings and commercial properties

Downside:

- Setup cost is high. The legal fees to setup each corporation are roughly $1,000 to $1,600 each
- Annual filing cost is likely around $750 to $1,000 for each corporation; need to make sufficient cash flow to cover the cost of annual filing. Best to make sure there is sufficient cash flow or appreciation for the filing
- Cannot prevent liability caused by landlord's gross negligence

Complete Taxation Guide to Canadian Real Estate Investing

- Personal guarantee on mortgage is likely required
- Qualification on mortgage can be more challenging with corporation

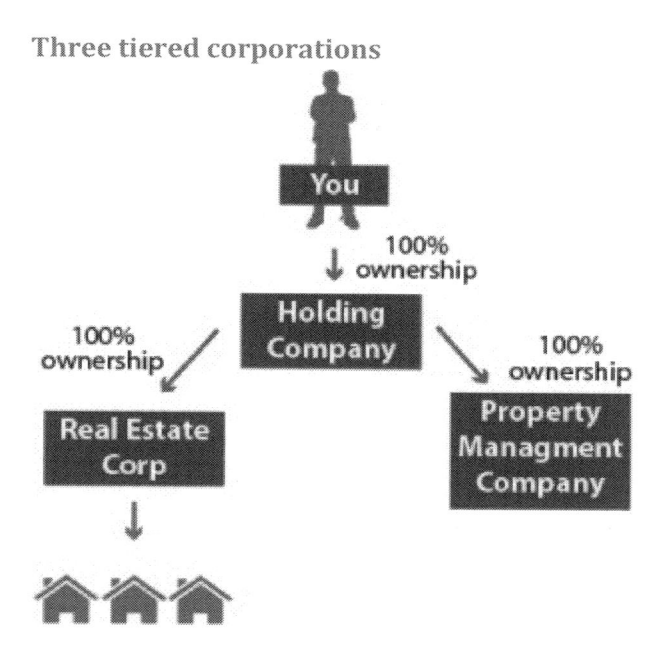

Three tiered corporations

```
                    You
                     |
                   100%
                  ownership
                     |
                 Holding
                 Company
          /                    \
      100%                     100%
    ownership               ownership
       |                         |
   Real Estate              Property
     Corp                   Managment
       |                     Company
       v
     🏠🏠🏠
```

Benefits:

- Protection against principle residence and personal assets from rental portfolio
- Able to convert a portion of the rental income into property management fees and enjoy a lower tax rate (46% vs. 15.5%)
- More money available for investing in Real Estate Corp.

- If investor is self-employed and earns income through Property Management Company, the after-tax money available to invest can be significantly more
- Tax planning opportunities available for income splitting with lower income spouse or other family members
- With proper planning, Real Corp. can have limited third party credit exposure
- With proven record of financial performance from properties and self-employed business, potential for the bank to allow the corporation to qualify for financing on its own without personal guarantee on the mortgage

Downside:

- Setup cost is high. Setup cost for each corporation roughly cost $1,000 to $1,600.
- Annual cost of filing is high. Annual cost of filing for each corporation by an accountant can range anywhere from $750 to a few thousand dollars.
- If tenant of one rental property sues the landlord, Real Co, for a large amount that insurance cannot covers, may affect other properties owned by Real Co.
- Cannot prevent liability caused by landlord's gross negligence
- Personal guarantee on mortgage is likely required
- Qualification on mortgage can be more challenging with corporation

These are the most common structures used by real estate investors who own a real estate portfolio in the corporations. You may question which structure makes most sense from a tax perspective. The answer is not always easy and it all depends on your own personal situation. I can definitely help you in recommending the most appropriate structure. Contact me to schedule a meeting to determine the best strategy for your own personal situation.

Commonly ask questions

Where should I start?

If you are first time investor and never owns any rental property before and you don't have a small business corporation, I would start with owning the property personally.

Try it out and see if you like being a landlord.

After all, the cost of setting up a corporation is about $2,000 plus HST charged by the lawyer.

Annual maintenance cost of a corporation would be about $1,000 plus HST as a minimum.

Not to mention the cost of running an extra corporation bank account and cost of maintaining a separate set of books.

But if you already got one and you are committed to building your rental portfolio as your retirement plan and prefer to utilize the flexibility of owning a property through the corporation, it is about time!

I would start with one corporation. Cost is lower and you can still test everything out.

Will the tax savings be worthwhile for me to setup the 3 tiered corporation? When would it make sense?

Three tiered corporations is one of the most common strategies real estate investors use. It is most effective when the investor owns a small business himself.

The cost of setting up the 3 tiered corporations is about $2,000 plus HST x 3 = $6,780.

Most investors would be lucky to have a cash flow of $6,780 from their first property, at least in the GTA market.

As a minimum, the cost of filing the tax returns for these corporations is more or less $3,000.

Say the after tax cost of the accounting fees is $2,000, this means that the tax savings have to be more than $2K a year to make it worthwhile to setup the 3 tiered corporations.

You would need at least 3 student rental properties to breakeven. Meaning that your tax savings is more or less the same as the cost of annual filing.

I have sufficient insurance coverage for the liability. I don't think corporations can help much to protect me.

Legal liability is also a big reason why people would incorporate. I once met with a real estate investor that just inherited $800K from her parents. She herself also owns her home with her husband that's worth over $800K and she has about $500K savings in RRSP.

Her net worth before incorporation was $2.1M. Is that a sufficient reason for her to incorporate?

Yeah, I know insurance can cover a lot of things, but insurance policy also comes with a lot of fine print.

I would definitely incorporate if it was up to me.

My mom's house recently had a pipe burst. The house was under renovation at the time it happened. We visited the property every few days but there's still a pipe burst.

The location of the pipe burst was from the second floor master bedroom bathroom. So a portion of the main floor ceiling fell. The main floor hardwood was all soaked in water and there was about 5 inches of water in the basement having nowhere to go.

Needless to say, the walls were all soaked in the main floor. Moisture from the pipe burst caused the paint to peel off and the door and window trims to buckle up.

Entire basement, which was newly renovated, was damaged.

The restoration company brought in 20 fans to dry up the entire place. The entire basement was stripped down to the stud.

All appliances were all found to be damaged.

Kitchen was also removed to dry up the wall. Kitchen cabinets were swollen as well.

Our insurance company initially denied the claim, on the basis that the property was vacant at the time. (Renovation was just finished and we were waiting for the new tenants to move in.)

We would have to be personally responsible for the 6 figure damage.

I didn't have the entire insurance policy with me. So I requested a copy of it at the time when I notified the insurance company.

Today, nearly a month after the incident happened, they still had not sent me the insurance policy.

Thankfully, because the property was under construction (the renovation was extensive enough that they would consider the property under construction), it was not considered vacant.

Thankfully, we visited the property often enough that the exclusion from the pipe burst section also would not apply.

So we eventually got the coverage.

You may think that it would never happen to you. WRONG!

You may think that the insurance will cover it. DEPENDS on the fine print!

Insurance may be sufficient to cover some liability, but definitely not all of it.

If something happened to your properties, your insurance won't cover it and you don't have the money to pay for it, you can sell your property and pay it off.

What if the sale proceeds aren't sufficient enough to cover the liability? The debtors can go after your personal assets if you own the property in your own name!

I'm not writing this to scare you. You don't know what you don't know.

That's what the corporation legal protection is for.

If you own commercial properties (such as commercial plazas, office buildings and industrial buildings), I would definitely incorporate.

I once managed 3 commercial plazas in South Western Ontario. One day, a pedestrian called requesting for compensation because she claimed that she slipped and fell in one of our plazas.

We called our snow removal guy immediately and asked him what's going on.

He checked the day log and discovered that there was no snow that week. All the snow was cleared the previous week.

Just when you think that you would only see this happening on TV, it happens in our everyday lives.

That's part of doing business. Part of being in the real estate business!

We told the lady about our daily log and what we found out. We never heard from her again.

But what if our snow removal guy wasn't keep tracking of what's happening? What if we really got sued for millions of dollars?

Would you be confident enough that your insurance coverage would be sufficient to cover everything?

You can see the setup cost and annual filing cost as an unnecessary cost but you can also see the cost as protecting your own wealth.

Complete Taxation Guide to Canadian Real Estate Investing

Should you charge more than $30,000 of management fees in a 3 tiered corporation setting?

Property management is subject to HST. But if you are a small suppliers that do not generate more than $30,000 of revenue, you are not required to collect HST.

But once you're over, you are required to register for HST and collect HST on behalf of the government.

Residential rental is not subject to HST. This means that the landlords are not required to charge HST on residential rental but they are also unable to claim the HST they paid on services provided, such as HST on repairs and utilities.

When the 3 tiered corporation strategy is used and when your residential portfolio is large enough, you may be able to reach $30,000 easily.

But as soon as you go over $30,000, you immediately lost 13% of the benefit.

Needless to say there's extra filing obligation for HST.

But if you are in commercial, you may be able to get exempted on the HST filing obligation. Even if you can't get away for not collecting HST, you would still be able to recover it.

Be aware that there's a maximum benefit you can achieve if you were to setup a 3 tiered corporation.

Cherry Chan, CPA, CA

Small business owners & real estate investors: 5 tips to structure your portfolio properly

One of the most asked questions I get is - should I setup a three tiered corporation? If so, what's the breakeven number?

Here are some tips to get you the answer.

1. **Do you have a small business?**

    Having a small business that's earning active income can get you ahead a lot faster.

    You earn your income inside a corporation and pay only 15% tax for the first $500,000 net income.

    If you earn $100,000 salary, you net roughly $75K after paying income tax.

    If you earn $100,000 from your business income inside a corporation, you pay $15,000 of tax and you can potentially pay close to zero dollar of taxes in your personal name with proper planning.

    If you decide not to take the money out from the corporation, you can invest within your corporate structure. You have so much more after tax money available within your corporation to invest. In our example, we are talking about $10K a year with $100,000 income.

2. **Do you need all the cash flow from your small business**

Complete Taxation Guide to Canadian Real Estate Investing

If you own a small business that's bringing in cash flow, three tiered corporate structure (or a variation of such) is almost the top advice I give to my clients.

But if you need all the money from your business for your personal expense, such as children's private school tuition fees and finance a boat you enjoy, you probably aren't in a position to invest in real estate at all.

Instead of setting up a corporate structure, I would highly recommend that you sit down and draft out a realistic income and expense statement and have a realistic picture of your financial situation.

Something gotta give before having enough money to invest in real estate.

I've once had a consultation with a couple who put their two kids in private school, own their own home in Markham/Richmond Hill through a mortgage and they also have a motorcycle to pay for (as a third vehicle).

They both made decent money and the wife is an accountant owning her own practice in a corporation as well.

They came in to see if I had a magic wand, but we, as accountants, only have a few tricks to save you taxes.

And taxes are a part of it but not everything.

Private school tuition for young kids, principal residence mortgage and a third motor vehicle in your family – these are all the expense items that would have to be paid for using your after tax money in your personal name.

These are personal lifestyle choice. I can't help you to make more money to finance these items.

I can only help you save a few bucks of taxes and invest more efficiently.

3. **Are you making cash flow from your properties yet?**

    When you are running a business, it is always a smart idea to lead your business with profit.

    This means that if your portfolio generates very little cash flow, you may not have the money to pay for the accounting fees.

    Assuming that you don't have a small business to begin with, setting up a 3-tiered corporation require a relatively large amount to set up. You would also need to pay your accountants annually to file the tax returns.

    If your portfolio consists of a few cash flow or even negative cash flow properties, you don't even have enough cash flow from your properties to pay for the accounting fees.

    The structure is designed in a way to save you taxes. Negative cash flow properties probably do not have much income to begin with. In turns defeating the purpose of using a 3-tiered corporate structure.

4. **How much time do you have to do all the work?**

As with all tax strategies, it takes time and effort to implement.

If you have a full-time job and setup a traditional three-tiered corporation to run your rental portfolio, the structure can help you save faster and invest faster.

But this comes with a cost.

First and foremost, it is a tax planning strategy. Like all tax planning strategies, it can be subject to CRA's scrutiny.

Secondly, to implement this strategy, you need to do regular invoicing, money must change hands on a periodic basis, documentation must be kept for all the property management work performed.

An accounting journal entry at year-end just wouldn't fix everything unfortunately.

How much time in your life do you have to implement this 3-tiered structure properly?

5. **Do you own 4 properties?**

    Many investors ask me when it would be a good time to setup a three-tiered structure.

    For small business owners, it's simple. Pretty much you should set it up as soon as you start your first rental property.

    For those of you who have full time job, the answer can be tricky.

I did a breakeven analysis and learned that for most people, if you own 3 to 4 rental properties, a three-tiered structure likely would pay for itself.

This means that if you own 3 to 4 properties, a 3-tiered structure won't get you any ahead. You, on the other hand, would have spent lots time drafting up invoices and implementing the strategy.

If you goal is to purchase 3 to 4 rental properties, you don't need the 3-tiered structure.

If you goal is to build a bigger portfolio, yes, by all means, go ahead. Just keep in mind that this will take you a few years to recoup and it is a long-term investment.

In summary, if you are a small business owner or a realtor, and would like to purchase a few investment properties, 3-tiered corporate structure is the way to go.

If you work full time and have no intention to leave your job, you may want to own properties in one or two corporations before upsizing it to a three-tiered structure.

Transfer properties to corporation can be expensive

Many investors are hesitant to incorporate at the beginning. They don't want to pay for the costs of incorporation, they don't want to pay for the cost of filing your corporation tax returns annually.

Before you know it, you may already have five properties in your own personal name. Now all of a sudden, you realize the benefit and flexibility you have from owning properties in a corporation.

What can you do?

With the existing properties, you can choose to do nothing with them or you can choose to transfer them into a corporation.

Here are the price tags of transferring the properties to the corporation.

1. Land transfer tax

   When you transfer the ownership to the corporation, even though in essence, you are transferring from your right pocket to left pocket, the law does not necessarily look at it the same way.

   Corporation is considered as a separate legal entity from you, despite the fact that you may be the sole shareholder of the company.

   As a result, the transfer of the title from you to the corporation will trigger land transfer tax.

And the land transfer tax is calculated at the fair market value.

One of my clients who is at his retirement age has multiple properties in the heart of Toronto. Most of us know that Toronto has double in land transfer tax.

He would like to minimize his future estate taxes. One strategy is to own these properties in a corporation.

To transfer all his personally owned properties in a corporation, he would have to pay tens of thousands of dollars in land transfer tax.

All of a sudden, the amount of land transfer tax suddenly makes the cost of setting up a corporation and maintaining them for years seem small.

If you are a long-term real estate investors and you are committed, you should consider investing in a corporation from the very beginning.

2. Capital gain tax

When you are transferring the title to the corporation, you are really selling the property to a separate entity.

This can potentially trigger capital gain tax.

For the people who have incurred large amounts of capital loss from investing in Nortel, selling the property at fair market value to trigger the capital gain can be desirable, as you can utilize the capital loss available to offset against the capital gain.

The corporation then has a larger amount of cost base. When it sells to a third party eventually, the capital gain can be lowered.

But if you don't have any capital losses carried forward, there is an election in the Income Tax Act that allows you to defer all the gain until you sell the property to a third party.

These elections are complicated forms that you would have to hire a real estate accountant to complete. A lawyer is also involved in the process to transfer the title.

3. Accounting fees & legal fees

Depending on the complexity of your portfolio, the cost to file the elections can start from $1,000 and up.

To complete the transfer, a lawyer is required to assist you in changing the title.

4. Opportunity costs of lost tax benefits

For real estate investors who own an incorporated business, cost of not incorporating can be substantial.

Most small business owners pay 15% corporation tax rate. They can use left over money to invest.

If they were to take out the money, report the income in their personal names and purchase the properties in their own name, this can cost them as much as 30% additional tax.

For $100,000 profit, we are talking about $30,000 of tax deferral opportunities. In two years, you can accumulate enough in the corporate structure for the downpayment of a property.

For real estate investors who don't own a business, you may still lose the income splitting opportunities that you would otherwise have with a corporation.

When you are thinking about the ownership structure of the corporations, make sure you don't overlook these four costs before making your decision!

Complete Taxation Guide to Canadian Real Estate Investing

Would I setup a 3 tiered corporation myself?

One of my family members is a professional, who has his own clinic. He's not incorporated yet.

He is the sole breadwinner of the family.

He's got an adult child, who's still in post secondary school.

His wife also works in the clinic as well, making more or less $60K salary.

They are also real estate investors.

He probably nets about $400,000 to $500,000. (When I say net, it means the income after all the allowable deductions for tax purpose. This amount is the taxable amount that is subject to personal tax.)

Don't get me wrong. I have a lot of respect for him and his work ethics. But when it comes down to tax planning, he's really years behind.

Let's use the following example to illustrate.

	Husband	Wife	Daughter	Total Family
Income	400,000.00	60,000.00	—	460,000.00
Tax	181,974.00	11,370.00	—	193,344.00
Net	218,026.00	48,630.00	—	266,656.00

Husband pays about $182K of tax on his net income of $400K. This $182K includes $5,089 CPP contributions (both employer and employee).

Wife pays about $11,370 of income tax.

Daughter can only make whatever she works for. Payment to daughter can be restricted and has to be reasonable based on the amount of work the daughter works in the clinic. In this case, the daughter does not work in the clinic and can't earn any salary.

So their combined family income is $460K, tax is $193,344, net with $266,656.

Let's start this ALL OVER AGAIN with a CORPORATION.

If the husband incorporates to hold his practice and opts to split income with his wife & his daughter using dividend, the company will have to first pay taxes on all the income.

	Corporation
Income	462,544.30
Corporation tax	69,381.65
After tax available for dividend	393,162.66
Dividends declared	200,000.00
After tax income to invest in corporation	**193,162.66**

Note that the income inside the corporation is higher since we are opting to pay the wife a dividend instead of salary.

	Husband	Wife	Daughter	**Total Family**
Dividend	100,000.00	60,000.00	40,000.00	**200,000.00**
Tax	16,007.73	4,599.08	907.93	**21,514.74**
Net	83,992.27	55,400.92	39,092.07	**178,485.26**

Yep, after receiving the dividend income from the corporations for $200K, the family pays only $22K of tax netting $178K to spend.

Of course, this dividend income can go up or down, depending on how much they would need for their personal expenses.

Complete Taxation Guide to Canadian Real Estate Investing

Also, the money left inside the corporation to purchase properties is $193K, the money left personally after paying taxes is $178K, a combined total of $371K.

If you compare $371K to $267K after tax income when he reports everything in his own personal names, there's a difference of $100K!!!! Per year!

This is the downpayment of one house, per year!

So why does he not incorporate?

Because the Canadian tax system is designed in a way that a taxpayer would pay the same amount of taxes whether you earn it in your corporation or in your personal name, he believes he would be paying the same amount of taxes regardless, so why bother?

Many entrepreneurs use their corporation as a way to retire, especially for those professionals who are not able to sell their business.

So instead of owning investment properties in your own names, you buy them in the corporation's names.

When husband retires in 20 years, he can slowly take the money out from his corporations via dividends.

This can add up significantly. In fact, it is $100,000 per year difference.

If he uses all his money in the corporation to purchase houses ($193,162 per year), he is able to purchase two properties a year.

Cherry Chan, CPA, CA

If he simply earns 10% interest on an investment fund, he can accumulate as much as $12M in 20 years before tax. $12 million dollars!

That's the difference he's not seeing.

My conclusion: If you have a small business, incorporate to invest. You have so much tax deferral opportunities available!

Complete Taxation Guide to Canadian Real Estate Investing

Resources

An Offer from Cherry Chan

For readers of *Complete Guide to Canadian Real Estate Taxation*

Dear Real Estate Investors,

This can be the end or a beginning. If you found value here, and hopefully find me to be interesting and engaging, you can sign up for my weekly Real Estate Tax Tips newsletter **for free**.

What you've seen here is one piece of the entire puzzle, I will continue to research on the latest tax strategies, tax updates and court cases.

I share all my research and experience on my weekly Real Estate Tax Tips newsletter every Thursday.

You will also receive invitation to in person seminar and webinars that I teach real estate taxes live.

You can enroll by visiting:

> www.RealEstateTaxTips.ca

Manufactured by Amazon.ca
Bolton, ON